Wake Up!

Daily Lessons for a
More Liberated and Loving Life

Wake Up!

Daily Lessons for a
More Liberated and Loving Life

Tom Owen-Towle

www.AperionBooks.com

APERION BOOKS™
1611A South Melrose Dr #173
Vista, California 92081
www.AperionBooks.com

10 9 8 7 6 5 4 3 2
First Edition 2013
Printed in the United States of America

ISBN-10: 0-9856039-1-7
ISBN-13: 978-0-9856039-1-5

Library of Congress Catalog Card Number: 2012953320

Cover & book design by CenterPointe Media
www.CenterPointeMedia.com

Dedication

To my beloved soul-mate, Carolyn . . .
our marriage continues to furnish my
dearest and most challenging
wake up calls!

Introduction

"I love Jesus who said to us:
Heaven and earth will pass away.
When heaven and earth have passed away,
My word will remain.
What was your word, Jesus?
Love? Forgiveness? Affection?
All your words were one word:
Wakeup."
—Antonio Machado

Who am I? Who are you? And who are we called to be, at this juncture in time, in this corner of the universe? Well, we've got some help in answering these ageless, imponderable questions. The spiritual giants in human history resoundingly offer a similar jumpstart: wakeup, wake up, wake-up. Whether or not wakeup is one word, as Machado poetically describes, two words as is commonly found, or a hyphenated word when used as an adjective…this concept stands as a worthy admonition for deepening the spiritual quest. Wake up is an essential mantra for our daily living.

According to tradition, a person once asked Gotama, "Are

you a god?" "No," he replied. "An angel?" "No." "A saint?" "No." "Then who or what are you?" And Gotama answered: "I am awake." Hence, Gotama became the Buddha, an awakened one. Note *an*, not *the*, awakened one. Hence, the Buddha-nature is inherent in every living creature. Buddha comes from the Sanskrit root *budh*: "to fathom a depth, to penetrate to the bottom, to perceive, to come to one's senses, to wake up."

Buddha was a pilgrim of unbounded energy who trudged the dusty roads of India for nearly half a century, calling women and men to wake up: moreover, to stay awake…journeying with ears and eyes, minds and hearts wide open. Buddhism formally began with a person who shook off the haze of life's fog. It continues every time any one of us wakes up to the entirety of our singular existence.

To be sure, splendid spiritual work is often accomplished or, at least fertilized, while we're asleep or daydreaming. And occasional naps are crucial. But too many of us are prone to narcotize ourselves rather than practice the art of being an awakened one. Wakefulness isn't a four-week intensive or even a five-year plan; it's the supreme way of being free and responsible humans during our lifetime.

Wake Up! Daily Lessons for a More Liberated and Loving Life is compiled for women and men who seek greater illumination and clarity. *Wake Up!* aspires to make us smile, open a few stuck doors, rouse us from a moral slumber, make our days and nights more bearable and beautiful…simply keep us in a state of conscious, deep awareness.

I resonate with the sentiment of the renowned American reformer and educator, Felix Adler (1851-1933), who, toward the close of his life, wrote: "I am grateful for the Idea that has used me." You hold in your hands a sourcebook of ideas or pieces of wisdom that have either soothed or tormented me throughout my own odyssey. Here are proven lessons that have sustained my wakefulness, day in and day out.

Forty-five years of writing sermons, giving talks, and leading workshops have certainly provided me with an abundance of useful material. The following notes, quotes, and anecdotes have filled myriad personal journals, file folders, and scrapbooks. Retirement from settled ministry furnished the golden opportunity to shape this mass of accumulated observations. *Wake Up!* is the result of a rigorous process of paring and polishing copious texts into more readable and accessible reflections–longer than tweets but shorter than protracted essays.

As a bona fide elder in his early 70's, I feel that now is a propitious time for me to sum up my core life-maxims and morals, then pass them on to others. I want my soul to be spent and my material and spiritual stuff either to be wisely lent or graciously sent. Like George Bernard Shaw, I intend my life "to be thoroughly used up when I die." I didn't say wasted or exploited, squandered or martyred, but "used up." I wish my body, mind, and heart to be employed in service of the highest and loveliest I have known. I'm not alone; I bet you do too. May *Wake Up!* serve that purpose.

Collecting, classifying, then conveying one's basic life-lessons via words is an effort to leave some sort of lasting legacy. Writing your values down in black-and-white becomes a bold act of self-transcendence.

Of course, so is having offspring. When I became a grandfather back in 1996, my driving desire for some form of continuation, call it immortality if you will, was palpable. I felt graced with a chance to embody a rekindled sense of grandness, even grandeur. Consequently, most everything I've composed in recent times has been crafted with my descendants in mind. How might my spoken and penned words assist little ones in becoming finders and bringers of liberation and love?

There already exist splendid collections that index principles and perspectives, both ancient and current, secular and spiritual. What makes *Wake Up!* different, maybe curious, is the fact that I've emphasized unconventional–even quirky and edgy–tests for a healthier and more mature life. I've tried to offer instructions and invitations that wouldn't normally be found in current self-help volumes or through Googling or Wikipedia searches for spiritual fulfillment.

Yet as fresh and innovative as one tries to be, every reader will inevitably stumble upon BFO's ("blind flashes of the obvious") in *Wake Up!* as well as now and again entertain a few moments of unpredictable illumination. No extant volume will cover every noteworthy lesson.

Millions of "wellness" advocates across America are currently outdoors, bright and early, revving up their cardiovascular engines for life's speedway. Yet we're overlooking the fact that our minds need limbering up every bit as much as our bodies. We need to shape our moral muscles and tone our consciences too. Our psyches hunger to be fortified daily with ample spiritual iron, for we are whole beings. Therefore, we require readable, digestible, and achievable exercises for traversing both the difficult and delightful passages of our existence. That is, if we truly desire to Wake Up!

Over the nearly five decades of my professional life, I have shared several of these *Wake Up!* challenges with friends and clients alike. And I've found that folks—when given a specific invitation or doable exercise every day—are motivated to stretch their minds and recharge their spiritual batteries, sometimes making attitudinal and behavioral changes, however small, on that very day. Daily exercising empowers us to feel better about ourselves, make a genuine difference at work, become more conscious citizens, as well as deepen our love-bonds.

So here are some easy and effective ways to use this daily regimen and reap proven benefits of spiritual fitness.

- Read each lesson, then close with moments of quiet reflection or prayer. Or peruse each contribution several times during the day, gaining different perspectives with each engagement. As Goethe put it: "One ought, every day at least, to hear a little song, read a good poem, see a fine picture, and, if possible, speak a few reasonable words."

- Consider writing your own commentary in the margin or compose your own inspirational text, maybe even a rebuttal. Or these lessons might spur interest in personal journaling.
- Use the ideas contained in *Wake Up!* as chow for conversation with family members around the breakfast or dinner table. Dining-and-talking together as a family is a rare and precious activity in today's fast-food, microwave world. Our children will simply consume as much as they're able.
- Consider closing your day by reading these life-affirming exercises to help clear unresolved angers and lingering clutter. *Wake Up!* is also eminently usable for staff meetings at work, spiritual friendship circles, or in the larger world. And how about processing the same lesson that your partner or friend reads, at different times, then planning moments for sharing when your paths rejoin?
- Study the same lesson each day as a buddy or family member living in a different part of the world; this can create bonding and a spiritual embrace across the miles. Or you can periodically share wake up calls via Skype!

One final tip, my friend. Feel free to use your imagination in reading *Wake Up!* Naturally, you may use this collection on a day-by-day basis in the order the lessons are presented. Or, you may wish to read them in a completely random manner, as the spirit moves you. There is simply no single, right way to "wake up."

For what they're worth, here is an entire year's worth of lessons that have "used me" and hopefully might use you. The sole aim of this book is to awaken oneself while healing our world.

From my heart, straightway to yours.
—Tom Owen-Towle

1

"Give Birth to Dancing Stars"

*"There must be enough chaos in one's
life to give birth to dancing stars. "*
—FRIEDRICH NIETZSCHE

Anaximander, the 6th century BC Greek philosopher, contended that the first principle of existence denotes a primordial realm of pure potentiality continually yielding fresh creation.

What might this basic principle mean for our daily lives? Well, we may rise in the morning with a plan in place, even specific tasks lined up, but, to be fully alive, we're challenged to open our hearts to the path of aperion: namely, to wake up to an infinite array of surprises. As Nietzsche rightly urges: "There must be enough chaos in one's life to give birth to dancing stars."

2
Seek Help When in Need

"Healthy, strong individuals ask for help when they need it,
whether they have abscesses on their knees or in their souls."
—RONA BARRETT

We self-sufficient, "type-A" Westerners seek help only in desperation. Consequently, we often muddle into endless trouble. When our car doesn't run right, we take it straightway to the garage. When our roof is leaking, we phone a repair person on the spot. When our head aches, we take a pain reliever. Yet when our spirits are scuffling or frayed, we hesitate to ask for aid.

Strong people seek succor amid difficulty or distress.

3
Stay Clear of Absolutes

"How can I believe in God when just last week I got my tongue caught in
the roller of an electric typewriter? I am plagued by doubts. What if every-
thing is an illusion and nothing exists? In that case, I definitely overpaid
for my carpet. If only God would give me some clear sign—like making a
large deposit in my name at a Swiss bank."
—WOODY ALLEN

After we stop laughing, we recognize the human hunger for certitude. Yet absolutes allow one to be absolved of the contingencies that make life a ragged yet exhilarating trek. Absolutes lead to absolution: they wipe out the nagging insecurities inherent in being

---

fully human. They also squeeze the juices out of reality.

Whoever is wary of submitting any question, secular or religious, to the test of open and free debate is more infatuated with their own opinions than with anything resembling truth. I recommend conducting a progressive (ever-advancing) life, unafraid to hold its wisdoms tentatively.

We're obliged, in this rapidly shifting world, to live our lives thinking and judging on the basis of incomplete and temporary knowledge. All of which spells adventure, risk, and creative unease.

I wouldn't want it any other way. How about you?

4

We Were Born for Improvisation

The great musician Jascha Heifetz was recorded on film playing his violin. When they analyzed his fingering in slow motion, it was learned that Heifetz was making continual, minute adjustments on the violin fingerboard.

As Heifetz was playing, he had to adjust his musical pitch, so, at some level, consciously or unconsciously, Jascha was constantly playing "slightly out of tune." Nobody noticed and nobody cared, since the resultant music was beautiful.

Same for us, in all walks of life; we're flawed and foibled, clanking along, always playing slightly out of tune. The first key is to confess, then internalize, that reality; and the second one is to keep on making adjustments, whether playing an instrument, driving a car, forging a bond of love, running a meeting, visiting someone in jail, or…

We can practice our instruments in private or even obtain a few lessons on the side, but most of the time we're like musicians improvising on a public stage. Personally, I think predestination is a lousy doctrine. I choose to edit and free lance all my days and nights.

5
"Thou Shall Not Commit Adultery"

The complexity of human love in today's world can't be contained in any simple dictum. Adultery, in a profound sense, is a private matter, not something for public legislation or tribal law. One thing I've learned, sometimes the hard way, over my 45 years of professional counseling, is this: never hastily judge the inner life or decision-making of another individual or couple.

To add to the confusion and ambiguity, even shady humor of it all, Moses went up the mountain to shape and receive the Decalogue, when he had two wives; then he came down without altering his own marital situation. Talk about a double message. But life is blemished, and so are both our religious sages as well as our living commandments.

Nonetheless, the kernel of this commandment challenges us, in our human friendships and loves, to be careful not to adulterate, shortchange, or compromise life's central vow of enduring loyalty and love. The seventh commandment claims that fidelity remains the most rewarding way to mature a bond of primacy and intimacy. That's certainly proven true in my adult life.

There's no way around it: fidelity costs ample energy, sacrifice, and staying power.

6
Quit Clinging

Mary Magdalene, who loved Jesus very much, is said to have seen him after his resurrection, and she immediately ran up to him. And Jesus said, "Do not touch me," but the Greek word *hatir* means "to cling to." In effect, Jesus said, "Don't cling to me, Mary!"

Don't cling to water, because the more you grab it, the faster it will slip through your fingers. Don't cling to your breath; you will get purple in the face and suffocate. You have to let your breath out. That's an act of supreme faith, to breathe out, believing that your breath will come back.

The religious journey is the art of knowing how to touch without clinging, of knowing when to connect and when to release.

7
Build an Affirmation File

A dear friend of ours recently disclosed a defining moment in her career. A competitor for her job came to Betty two years later and inquired: "Do you have an affirmation file?" "What's that?" Betty asked. "Well, it's a file in your work cabinet that's filled with constructive, heartfelt compliments from clients and fellow workers... kudos that celebrate the core of your character. Whenever you receive such unsolicited affirmations, you place them in a file (under A), right at the front of your cabinet. Then, on days when you're depleted, frustrated, even prone to say, 'I can't do this work anymore!' go directly to your affirmation file and soak in some honest and glowing praise."

Then this competitor turned to our friend and said: "And today, Betty, I want to start building your file with my own proof of the splendid work you're doing," and she gave Betty her first affirmation for the file, which, by the way, is bulging.

Without affirmations from others, we wither and sputter. With affirmations, we flourish...as long as we're able to take them to heart.

8
Find Places to Be Alone

*"A human being who has not a single hour for
their own every day is no human being."*
—RABBI MOSHE LEIB

There's a crucial distinction between being *alone*, which is being comfortable with our solitude, and being *lonely*, which indicates unwholesome apartness from other living beings. We need to embrace aloneness while diminishing loneliness.

Creative solitude is the prelude to fruitful communion. Indeed, the best way to battle debilitating isolation is not merely through activity or companionship but through immersion in being quiet and still. Our inner soul can prove to be quite a resourceful compadre, if regularly visited.

Imagination and camaraderie are fertilized during periods of our aloneness.

9
Heed the Lure of the Cry

"Blowing through heaven and earth, and in our hearts and the heart of every living thing, is a gigantic breath, a great Cry, which we call God..."
—Nikos Kazantzakis

As we humans continue our evolution, the Cry perseveres as well. It beckons us to superior emotional growth, intellectual integrity, and spiritual awakening. We can't let go of the terra firma, since we are incurable earthlings, but, while remaining grounded, we can aspire upward and onward. Indeed, we stagnate if we fail to tune into the Cry.

The Cry summons us to keep on budding and blossoming for our own benefit and for the good of the entire cosmos.

10
Become a Both/Andian

"To brave people, good and bad luck are like a right and left hand. They use both."
—St. Catherine

You and I must be flexible enough to handle both our trials and our triumphs. We can't predict what external forces will invade our lives. We need to utilize whatever fortune comes our way. Bravery spells interior strength.

Many of us cater to the natural hand and shy away from our minor one. We turn to our normal places of power and skirt our irksome weaknesses. The courageous among us dare to employ both hands with equal dexterity.

An illustration. A Sufi master was strolling through the streets one day with his devotees. When they arrived at a city square, a ferocious fight was being waged between government troops and rebel forces. Terrified by the bloodshed, the students implored: "Master, quick, which side should we help?"

"Both," the master replied, "both."

As my friend, Jaco, challenges: become a both/andian!

11
We Are Meaning-Makers

"We should look at meaning as seriously as we look at the cholesterol level or the blood pressure. Meaning enters the body and makes the difference in many cases of life and death."
—LARRY DOSSEY

Any task we do can be monotonous or worthless. It only comes alive and conveys joy when we treat it as special and sacred. Meaning lies not in something but in what we bring to that something. We are meaning-makers, you and I.

Novelist J. D. Salinger has Zooey say to his sister Franny that no prayer is going to save her until she can recognize *consecrated* as different from *concentrated* chicken soup. The difference lies in how the water is added, how it's heated, and how it's served. It's the act of making concentrated into consecrated chicken soup that blesses both the one who prepares and the one who consumes.

It's time to enjoy some CCS for lunch, for life!

12
Avoid Booby Prizes

In all of our important encounters, being gratified or happy beats being right or correct anytime. Victory isn't the aim of love, fulfillment is; so when we chase the elusive and erosive goal of being right, we often end up with a booby prize.

Put similarly, we are obsessed with *finding* the right friend or right mate, when we should be aspiring to *be* the right friend or right mate ourselves. All we can accomplish, in the final analysis, is being the best possible version of ourselves or, as my friend says, resembling the person my dog thinks I am.

Pass up booby prizes whenever possible.

13
Maintain Your Balance

"We always travel along precipices.
Our truest obligation is to keep our balance."
—JOSE ORTEGA Y GASSET

Buddha was an advocate of the Middle Path. He felt that right disposition spelled composure of mind and stability of spirit, especially under trying circumstances. He wrote that the greatest word in any language was "equanimity."

Our tendency is to become distraught under strain or delirious amidst triumph. Of course, we're permitted to display lavish feeling during extreme moments, but an attitude of equanimity will hold us and others around us in good stead through all kinds of weather. Put similarly: nothing to excess, not even moderation!

I've always admired the Nobel Prize winner Linus Pauling, who acted with propriety and class in being invited to a White House dinner dance. He spent the day picketing the White House in opposition to American nuclear policy. Then he changed to a dinner jacket and spent the evening as the late President Kennedy's guest.

Pauling was a person with a sense of proportion or balance. May we follow in such footsteps.

14

Lean Far into Your Ancestors

"Let us lean far, far into our ancestors
until our eyebrows knit together."
—ZEN SAYING

The French writer Jean Lanier reflected upon the Jewish cemetery in Europe where his ancestors were buried. The cemetery had been closed for years; so they had to get a key to open the wrought-iron gate. The gravestones were overgrown with brambles, but eventually Lanier came upon the grave of his great-grandparents. Big, juicy strawberries grew on it, and he enthusiastically sampled them without his parents minding. "Only much later did I marvel at their good sense, letting their little son eat fruit nourished by the dust of his ancestors. Much of my attitude toward death and of my feeling of being part of a web of life came from that primal experience."

A similar snapshot pops to mind: we would hold an Easter morn service in the rustic canyon behind our church sanctuary. Early in the morning, before families arrived, we would hide Easter eggs amidst the brambled bushes on our plateau. After an intergenerational service of poignant sharing, the children were released to hunt for the eggs. This was the same canyon terrain where the cremains of congregational members, usually in private ceremonies, had been scattered over some fifty years.

Comparable to Lanier's graveyard, our church offspring would blithely come upon eggs mingled with the ashes of their spiritual ancestors…coming to grips, in child-like fashion, with the wisdom that life and death are intermingled, holy forces.

15
Change Thyself

"I doubt if anyone really wants to change his or her way of life, though all of us would like to make the bad feelings go away."
—RIC MASTEN

The Sufi Bayazid says this about himself: "I was a revolutionary when I was young and my prayer to God was: 'Lord, give me the energy to change the world!' As I approached middle age and realized that half my life was gone without my changing a single soul, I changed my prayer to: 'Lord, give me the grace to change all those who come in contact with me. Just my family and friends, and I shall be satisfied.' Now that I'm an old man and my days are numbered, I've begun to see how foolish I've been. My one prayer now is: 'Lord, give me the grace to change myself.' If I had prayed for this right from the start, I should not have wasted my life.'"

The striking fact is that if we really want to harbor enduring joy, then we must start and finish by working on ourselves. It's no easy enterprise, for one as mature as Gandhi always moaned that he had far more influence for the better upon the British nation or the Indian people than he did upon himself—his most formidable test.

16

Name Your Anchors

"One must not tie a ship to a single anchor or life to a single hope."
—Epictetus, Stoic philosopher (A.D. 55-135)

Popular knowledge reminds us to avoid tunnel vision. It's often the case that we give ourselves totally to just one cause, one love, one intention, and when that single anchor fails, our life is adrift. We are lost at sea.

In truth, there is no single hope that can sustain one's entire existence but rather an intricate cluster of wishes. Furthermore, what serves as an anchor at one time often fades, while others emerge in the foreground.

An anchor is something or someone who is a mainstay—a reliable or principal support—that will secure you firmly in place as your life prepares to soar. There's nothing flimsy or shaky about an anchor. An array of anchors is readily available to every one of us. Name three that shore up your voyage right now.

17

Welcome and Be Welcomed!

*"Let love continue. Do not neglect to show hospitality to strangers,
for thereby some have entertained angels unawares."*
—Hebrews 13: 1-2

Our ministers' group was holding a retreat at a Catholic center in upstate New York. One of the elderly nuns greeted us graciously at the outset of our weekend. As she completed her remarks, the

Sister mentioned that her order would retain a list of all of our names throughout the weekend. Furthermore, she wanted us to wear our names tags not only for ourselves but also for the nuns. Why? "Because when we see you, we want to call you by name. And every morning after chapel, I want you guests to know that we will be reading the entire list of your names, then offering a special prayer of support and guidance for each of your days. Welcome to St. Joseph's Retreat Center!"

I've rarely felt more welcomed in my whole life.

18
Be Angry for Impact Not Injury

"When angry, count to 10 before you speak;
if very angry, 100."
—THOMAS JEFFERSON

Sometimes when we're angry, it's wise to share our upset immediately rather than "sit on it," lest our anger degenerate into rage or acts of unintentional damage. Anger can be a charitable emotion that chastens or confronts in order to restore community. Hostility, on the other hand, is the attempt to demean or destroy. Wisdom lies in distinguishing between the two.

Other valuable reminders concerning our anger:

- Bottled wrath can result in depression.
- Vent wisely, since a wanton display of anger merely makes us angrier…turn your anger into a slow-burning, productive fire rather than an all-consuming blaze that might devour everything, including yourself…
- My friend says it's better to *make* a pot than *break* a pot when angry.

- Anger is not the opposite of love; apathy is…so anger can be a loving emotion, meaning that I care enough to give you the best of myself, including my upset. Your anger becomes what some call "intelligent rage." Anger is a blaze that burns, cleanses, and crackles in service of right relationship.

As Danann Perry illustrates: "Human beings are like volcanoes plugged at the top; when the lava is allowed to flow a bit at a time, it may burn up a few trees but it also makes a new land upon which new life can grow."

Currently, parents are prone to place their children in "time-out" whenever they bubble over with fury. Well, we adults might consider placing our own selves in time-out whenever our distress grows overwhelming.

19
Confess Your Bewilderment

Walt Whitman was attending a funeral one day. Just ahead of him a teenage girl of 14 was standing before the open casket as though she were transfixed. The literary giant put his arm on her shoulder and spoke to her. "You don't understand that, do you?" he asked gently. And as she honestly answered, "No," Whitman added, "Well, neither do I." And they moved on together.

None of us, of any age, can comprehend the premier, obdurate mysteries of existence such as love, evil, sexuality, or death. What unites us as companionable travelers is our willingness to huddle together—singing, dancing, weeping, and moaning—confessing our bewilderment and making plain the courage of our confusions.

20
"A Person Can Suffocate on Courtesy."
—JEROME LAWRENCE

This is the punch line in Lawrence's play *Inherit the Wind*, the story about the Scopes trial, the courtroom drama of the 20th century where the freedom of every American was at stake.

I believe in being courteous, gracious, and thoughtful. But, like all other virtues, you can overdo them. Too much courtesy smacks of saccharine. Nicey, nice! It can degenerate into faintheartedness.

There are moments when we should assert rather than defer, intervene and push back rather than submit. There are times in our personal interactions when we may be suffocating someone, including ourselves, with gobs of gooey courtesy.

21
Recognize the Souls of Animals

"To live as siblings with beast and flower not as oppressors."
—DENISE LEVERTOV

At different times in human history, we've denied soul to entire classes of beings whom we've wanted to control. Women, it was once said, had no soul. Slaves reportedly had no soul. Enemies are just numbers, without worth. And now, we perpetuate that illusory and degrading practice by treating ourselves as conscious subjects and all other animals as dumb objects.

We treat the beasts of the field, the birds of the sky, and the fish of the sea as unanimated, without soul, hence without enduring value. Yet the very word *animal* comes from a Latin root that means "soul." To ancient thinkers, soul was the mysterious force that gave life and breath to a myriad of the earth's creatures, but later theologians restricted the possession of a soul to human beings.

At long last, we're beginning to realize that all oppressions are interrelated and, moreover, when any one living reality is ignored, rendered disposable, or destroyed, the entire cosmos shudders and wails. Little by little, we're recognizing the plight of our nonhuman kin, the animals.

Clearly, not all animals are social or altruistic, nor can all distinguish between right and wrong, but isn't the same achingly true with respect to our human sisters and brothers? Given the state of humanity today, across the globe, might it be time to inquire whether or not *we* have souls?

With our immense powers of imagination and creativity humans can wipe out habitats of species that will go extinct forever or we can manage ways of respectful co-existence. We humans have that kind of power; we possess that measure of responsibility.

All living beings share the one blessed breath of Creation.

22
Spend Time with Antagonists

"Have you not learned great lessons from those
who dispute the passage with you?"
—WALT WHITMAN

Too often we read or engage only those ideas that massage our egos. We join mutual admiration societies, yet we mature the most when grappling with thinking wholly at odds with our own. The famous actor Lawrence Olivier refused to read the complimentary reviews of his plays but pondered in depth the stabbing critiques. "That way, I would always learn more!"

One of my seminary professors made it a compulsory assignment to write an essay on a theological adversary. Our task was to pinpoint the real, not just paper, strengths of our opponent and, more importantly, determine how their viewpoint might deepen our own.

I once saw a sign over a library magazine rack that read, "Warning: these periodicals may be hazardous to your point of view." We drift toward those articles that stroke our biases. When some statement unsettles us, we discount it as inaccurate reporting or shallow reflection. We finagle a prejudiced result.

Here's another angle. As my "liberal" colleague notes: "A window stuck open is as useless as a window stuck shut. In either case, you've lost the use of the window." Hence, our windows need to stay adaptable: opening and closing, moving up and down according to weather changes.

Fixed viewpoints help us see neither much nor far. Occasionally, liberals should be reading conservative materials and reactionaries dealing with radical appraisals. That way, our vision is more likely to expand than shrink.

23

Stand Ready to Apologize

"An apology is the superglue of life. It can repair just about anything."
—Lynn Johnston

Note the exchange between Calvin and Hobbes, the cartoon characters. Calvin says to Hobbes, "I feel so bad that I called Susie names and hurt her feelings. I'm sorry I did it." "Well, maybe you should apologize to her," Hobbes suggests. Calvin ponders this for a moment and then replies, "I keep hoping that there's a less obvious solution."

Well, there isn't a more direct or positive solution available than apologizing. I grew up with the familiar sentiment that erroneously claimed "love means never having to say you're sorry!" On the contrary, love means having the size of heart to say, on a regular basis, "I'm sorry, I apologize," in order to restore a broken bond.

An apology doesn't erase the past, but it can furnish both parties with a more satisfying future.

24
"Drive Away Temptations and Distractions..."

*"If at prayer we do nothing but drive away temptations
and distractions, our prayer is well made."*
—St. Francis de Sales

Whether we meditate a few minutes per day or contemplate for hours, we anticipate earth-shaking results. We would be wiser to appreciate modest returns. Any release from tension during our frantic lives is refreshing. It doesn't take much to grant serenity for facing the grueling moments up ahead.

A gauge of our spiritual strength is discoverable in the number of distractions and disturbances we repel daily. Prayer can furnish a fruitful wake up call.

25
Ground Yourself!

*"I cannot have a spiritual center without having a geographical one.
I cannot live a grounded life without being grounded in a place."*
—SCOTT SANDERS

Every day we get out of bed, we might ask ourselves a series of telling and linked queries: Where in the world am I? More specifically, where in my life am I? And am I where I desire to be, need to be, am called to be? Once we sort out where we choose to be, the next step is to be fully present and accounted for on that local hunk of turf.

Here's my prayer: as religious pilgrims may we remain grounded on the earth while touching the sky; may we employ to the fullest the one body, the one spirit, the one conscience with which we have each been uniquely blessed; and may we never lust after another's profession or hopelessly imitate the soul of our neighbor.

When I come to the conclusion of my earthly sojourn, offers the Talmud, I will not be asked why I wasn't Moses, but why I wasn't Tom Owen-Towle, the fullest version of my singular being. And every one of you will be asked the very same question.

It has taken me the bulk of my 70+ years to realize that the likeliest path to the ultimate ground goes directly through my local ground: that means the land itself, the rivers and mountains, the stone outcroppings and the human neighbors, and all the plants and animals that share this particular ground.

San Diego is my ground, where I belong now: my tilling ground, my holy ground, my battleground, and my growing ground.

26

Applause Sometimes Comes Too Easily

The late Bishop Fulton J. Sheen was greeted by a burst of applause when he made his appearance as a speaker at a meeting in Minneapolis. Sheen responded by saying: "Applause before a speaker begins is an act of faith. Applause during the speech is an act of hope. Applause after they have concluded is an act of charity."

In today's human discourse, applause is delivered too facilely for my taste. It becomes a bromide. I would rather people express their spiritual *olé* with silence or a respectful wave of the hands. Of course, there exist times for outright ovations, but people currently clap at most everything that moves in front of them, making for too oily and slick an exchange.

Once when the radical feminist author Audre Lorde spoke, she was almost defiant when her audience began to clap. Lorde said, in effect, thanks but no thanks: "Applause is easy. I urge you instead to go out and do something."

27

Be Satisfied with Enough

"God has gifted us with everything that is necessary."
—HILDEGARD OF BINGEN

The Hebrew word *dayenu* means "enough." It's integral to the Jewish Seder ritual and part of the song that if God had only delivered us from Egypt, it would have been enough. If God had only given us the Torah, the five books of Moses, it would have been enough.

If God had only given us the Sabbath, it would have been enough.

What is enough for each of us? What are our critical needs: food, shelter, justice, love? What else would we desire as a staple in our diet? The truth is that not everyone has access to life's necessities—the raw material, the tools, and the disciplines to live a satisfying life; so it's our human mission to insure that what belongs to people gets to them.

The Buddhists claim that "enough is a feast." Then the question becomes: when is enough enough? When do we have a sufficient supply of life's basics so as to live as free and fulfilled women and men?

I close this lesson with a touching exchange between a father and daughter in their last moments together at the airport; the girl is going away to college and her father is dying.

Standing near the security gate, they hugged and the father said, "I love you, and I wish you enough." The daughter replied, "Dad, our life together has been more than enough. Your love is all I ever needed. On your next voyage, I wish you enough too, Dad!"

Dayenu!

28
"Appreciation Is a Wonderful Thing."

*"Appreciation is a wonderful thing. It makes what is
excellent in others belong to us as well."*
—Voltaire

Appreciation is the art of sensitive awareness: an expression of admiration and gratitude that increases the worth of something. I say art when I could just as easily have said skill. In any case, we live in a world where appreciation is under-practiced. People gravitate to being nasty and negative. A jaundiced eye is cast at much of life.

In Buddhism, there's an idiom that whenever you point a finger in criticism at another, three fingers are pointing back at you. In short, you perceive your own faults in others. Well, the same thing holds when we single out someone in appreciation; three fingers are pointing back at ourselves.

In appreciating another we create communion; we're bonded, we share in the exhibited excellence.

29

We Only Catch the Hind Parts of God

"God dwells in the prepositions: beyond, among, within, beneath."
—SHARON PARKS

Little Nancy was busy with her crayons. Her mother asked whose picture she was drawing? "God," Nancy replied. "But, my dear, nobody knows how God looks," the mother lovingly admonished. "They will when I'm finished," the child answered.

A charming story, but the mother is the wiser of the two in this instance.

As the second of the Ten Commandments claims: God is everlastingly impossible to represent. You can feel the spirit, but you can't capture its likeness. When we enter the most secret chamber of the tabernacle, the holy of holies, we will find it empty, because no image or picture or sculpture of the Eternal One can be made.

The Decalogue reminds us that we aren't gods ourselves nor is anything else God that we might create out of wood or words, clay or stone, anything we might wear around our necks or anything we might place on altars or dashboards. The Infinite transcends all that. The reality of God is beyond our creation, comprehension,

---

and control. Period. And we'll never do any better than Moses, who caught only an occasional glimpse of God's hind parts.

30
Avoid Arrogance

"Thank God I am not as other people."
—PHARISEE

High self-esteem undoubtedly pays off. Folks with a healthy amount of pride are happier, free of ulcers, and less prone to insomnia or addictions. But there exists an overweening pride that drives us to being rash, willful, and arrogant. This is referenced in the philosopher Bertrand Russell's piercing adage: "I am firm, you are obstinate, she is a pig-headed fool."

Researchers have discovered that under certain conditions most people will act in rather inconsiderate ways. When other people are told in detail about these conditions and asked to predict how *they* would act, nearly all insist that their own behavior would be far more virtuous.

Similarly, when social analyst Stephen Sherman called some residents in a certain location and asked them to volunteer three hours to an American Cancer Society drive, only 4% agreed to do so. But when a comparable group of other residents were called and asked to predict how they would react were they to receive such a request, almost 50% predicted that they would help.

Alas, our views of ourselves are more highfalutin than reality suggests. We imagine ourselves more gracious and generous than we end up being. We claim to be holier than we really are. We must walk the fine line between being proud and arrogant, *sure* of ourselves without being *full* of ourselves.

31

Possess an Astonished Heart

"Delight in your children openly. Look at them with the widest eyes you can manage and don't be ashamed to be seen at wonder. You will not see their likes again. What a shame if they should leave home without ever knowing they have been beheld and offered up by an astonished heart."
—ROBERT CAPON

We have countless gifts to exchange with our offspring. But no greater gift is more indispensable than beholding them with delight, wonder, and an astonished heart. It's our joyous duty to treat every child as an unrepeatable and growing enchantment. To behold them as such puts us in the behaving mood to treat them as such.

Unquestionably there exist ample frustrations, even cul-desacs, in parenting. I've experienced a slew of them personally. But through the sad and agonizing moments, may our parental affirmation and gratitude shine forth, for we shall never see their likes again.

32

Take Spiritual Stock

The ten-day period of Rosh Hashanah, according to Jewish tradition, is a time for repentance, prayer, and charity in preparation for the holiest date of the year, Yom Kippur, which means "The Day of Atonement." It serves as a wake up call, the season for repentance, stock-taking, spiritual clarity, and resolve for our lives.

On this day we seek forgiveness from gods, humans, animals, plus ourselves. Negotiating forgiveness, however, is not sufficient. Our wrongs must be righted, whenever possible. We need to undo our evils and conduct improved lives.

Rosh Hashanah is the time to ponder our purpose, to bring our identity and vision into closer alignment—our chance for soul-searching without breast-beating. Rosh Hashanah challenges us never to tolerate permanent estrangement from either ourselves or others. But such an unswerving commitment to reconciliation or inching ever closer toward at-one-ment with the Cosmos will take more than ten days.

It sounds to me more like a lifetime.

33
Be Present and Accountable

"You must be present to win."
—Las Vegas Casino

A mother is dutifully getting breakfast ready for her son on another school day. Hearing nothing, she proceeds to Herman's room, only to find him still in bed. "Herman, are you okay?" she asked. "I'm okay, but I'm not going to school today!"

She decided to challenge her lethargic, lazy son: "Well, then, Herman, give me three good reasons why you aren't going to school." "Okay, I don't like school; the teachers don't like me; and I'm afraid of the kids." "Alright" said his mother, "now I'm going to give you three good reasons why you are going to school. Number one, I'm your mother and I say school is important. Number two, you're forty-two years old. And number three, you're the principal of the school!"

Woody Allen claims that "80% of the successful life is showing up!" Allen is partially right, for it's the remaining 20% that gives us fits, separates those who merely appear and those who produce once they've shown up. So, here's the math: showing up is 80%; being attentive is 5%; responding fully is another 5%; and then remaining adaptable for unplanned shifts constitutes the final 10%. Then we can claim to be fully present and accountable.

34
May You Find a Sufficiently Good Match

The hopelessness of seeking perfection in love is illustrated by the Sufi story of Mullah Nasrudin who wanted to marry and had set out to find the perfect mate. First he traveled to Damascus, where he found a perfectly gracious and beautiful woman but discovered she was lacking a spiritual side.

Then his travels took him farther to Isfahan, where he met a woman who was deeply spiritual yet comfortable in the world and beautiful as well, but unfortunately, they didn't communicate well together. "Finally in Cairo I found her," he said, "she was the ideal woman, perfect in every way." "Well," asked a friend, "did you then marry her?" "No," answered the Mullah, "because unfortunately she was looking for the perfect man."

We're desperately and forlornly looking for the perfect job, the perfect partner, the perfect faith, the perfect body, and these passionless Platonic abstractions don't exist in reality. We're good and imperfect creatures called to build and sustain good and imperfect relationships, jobs, and communities.

Relational math warns us that half a person times half another person—however exceptional the individuals involved are—produces one-fourth of a bond. There are synergistic situations in which, as E. E. Cummings noted, "two plus two is five, at least." Relational math is funny. Two plus two equals five, if the situation is expansive and growing. Other times, two plus two equals eight or more because of the multiplying dynamics involved. Then again, two plus two might equal less than four because of the fractious, divisive effect of any given encounter.

Our goal needs to be wholeness not perfection. Whole people long to be with whole people. Whole persons are willing divulge their warts and weaknesses rather than hide them. They dance upon the razor's edge in pursuit of a loving bond. Whole people settle for a sufficiently good rather than a perfect match.

Start by being the partner you wish to have.

35
Pay Attention, Pay Attention, Pay Attention

I offer two illustrations of the importance of paying attention to one another, especially toward the little ones who inhabit our world.

First, a man who had been condemned to die in the electric chair was asked if he had a final statement to make. He looked at the many reporters, photographers, and officials who surrounded him and spoke plainly yet bitterly: "If I had been shown so much attention when I was a little boy, I promise you, I wouldn't be here today."

Here's a second story, less dramatic but equally relevant to mature parenting. A frustrated teenager is said to have complained to her school counselor: "You know what I am at home? I'm nothing but a comma. When I talk to my mother, she listens for a minute, then she starts walking away. She makes me a comma. It's as if I didn't say anything worthwhile."

In Zen Buddhism, we're reminded that in first place dwells the

virtue of "paying attention," then in second place
tion," and in third place is "paying attention." M
and impasses in life itself, as well as in our relation
paying insufficient attention.

Can you document this in your own journey?

36

"Life Must Be Understood Back But Lived Forwards."
—SOREN KIERKEGAARD

We need to remember the blunder we committed in March 2004,
so we won't repeat it. And December 1979 was a painful time to
endure; let us learn from it. The special joy we experienced in the
summer of 1991 has energized us for a long time. But we're entering an unknown epoch, and we're invited to reside there richly and
resourcefully. Remember what happened to Lot's wife when she
looked back; she turned into a pillar of salt and calcified.

As they say, if we don't learn from the mistakes of yesterday,
we're likely to repeat them. Likewise, if we don't mature from the
wisdoms of yesterday, we're liable to forget them. We need to understand and bless where we've been before we set out on any new
road.

The mythical African *Sankofa* bird faces backward but flies forward. It reminds us that we must reclaim our past so that we can
more deftly forge our futures.

Backwards and forwards, all the way home.

37
Cease Making Comparisons

A small shrub, growing next to tall pines, looked at the ground and said, "Look how tall I am." The tall pine in looking at the sky, sighed: "Look how short I am." Life's a matter of perspective, isn't it?

Comparisons of all sorts are inevitable. We're slower than some and faster than others. We're more or less agile communicators depending upon the company we keep. However, the value of comparisons is modest and short-lived. We would be wise to realize, once and for all, that we'll always be superior or inferior to someone, somehow, somewhere, and sometime. So, my counsel is to stop either groveling or boasting.

Life's bottom line is to be the finest edition of our idiosyncratic selves as possible.

38
Be a Friendly Persuader

"The dynamics of democratic leadership lie not in manipulation but in persuasion."
—Woodrow Wilson

Manipulation and exploitation are strategies that may harvest quick results, but lasting change cannot be coerced—only charmed. I've always admired John Woolman, the 18th-century Quaker who was devastated that some Quakers held slaves. To change this state of affairs he didn't censure the slaveholders. Woolman refused to ha-

---

rangue his compatriots; rather he resorted to friendly persuasion. Hence, he traveled on horseback, visiting each one individually and voicing his moral concern.

It took Woolman 30 years to sway all of them. But in the end not one Quaker owned a slave. Passing laws would probably have done the job but not without persistent bitterness. As prophetic leaders, our job is to transform people, not just enforce rules, always remembering that we won't necessarily be as triumphant as Woolman.

But we're called to be faithful, not successful.

39

It's Okay to Be a Barnacle

"The barnacle enjoys movement, the parasite knows life, and the hitchhiker does, or can, 'get there.' More positively, all three may be in range of something greater than what they would have known had they stayed home or unattached."
—MARTIN MARTY

This is a sobering thought for the incorrigibly free spirits among us who cling to independence as a terminal value. I too treasure human autonomy, the unfettered mind, and the self-possessed spirit. Nonetheless, we spiritual adventurers are seldom original in planning or executing our voyages. Others have journeyed before us. In one way or another, we're all parasites, hitchhikers, yea, barnacles.

Before we sing the praises of our own prowess, a debt of gratitude needs to be rendered to those rocks, ships, or people to whom and to which we've been temporarily or permanently barnacled.

Stay in Dialogue

"Dialogue is to love what blood is to the body. When the flow of blood stops, the body dies. When dialogue stops, love dies and resentment and hate are born. Indeed that is the miracle of dialogue."
—REUEL HOWE

By staying in dialogue, notice I say staying, our delights are multiplied and our burdens reduced. Without dialogue, friends and lovers are smoldering kegs of dynamite. With the miracle of shared communication, we possess the opportunity to enhance self, friend, and our third creation: the relationship.

In dialoguing, we are, as the poet Adrienne Rich stated, "trying to extend the possibilities of truth between us." Dialoguing proves to be a miracle, for we end up with more than we were before we entered the exchange. Nonetheless, as with all miracles, dialogue can be fleeting and frustrating unless sustained by human sweat. The marvel of communion with another rapidly fades without constant practice.

I've found in interpersonal relations—especially when any conversation reaches a tricky passage, even impasse—that there exist no more golden words to open up the soul of another than plainly to inquire: "Tell me more." No amplification is needed, just the phrase: "Tell me more."

One we regularly engage in *dia-logue* with another person, we can graduate to *poly-logue* with groups.

41
"Baseball Is a Lot Like Life."

*"Baseball is a lot like life. Line drives are caught,
the squibbers go for hits; it's an unfair game."*
—ROD KANEHL

Ted Williams, who grew up in our hometown of San Diego, was a troubled youth who possessed a passion for baseball. His teachers, realizing this state of affairs, allowed Ted to bring his bat to school as a "security blanket," while they labored to assist him in the arts of academia. Williams never developed into much of a student, but he did become one of the greatest pure hitters the game of baseball has ever known. Yet Ted Williams was successful only 30+ percent of the time. Baseball is surely one of life's all-time humblers.

Hitting stats are reinforced with team results as well. The worst team wins 35% of the time, the best team loses 35% of their games, and the other 30% determines who is ultimately victorious. Or as Ted Williams claims himself: "Don't you know how damn hard hitting a baseball is?"

42
"Every Morn Is the World Made New."

"A fresh beginning; every morn is the world made new."
—SARAH WOOLSEY

My faith declares that we're wondrous yet fiercely flawed, ever renewable creatures. Our ability to grow and to make strides is the most important claim to be made about us earthlings. When we ignore or fail to trust in our capacity to start over, we invariably succumb to feelings of despond.

"Every morn is the world made new." Each moment is a place we've never visited before. The question of Zhao-Zhou furnishes a daily test: "Do I use my 24 hours or am I used by them?" Fellow-travelers: I invite you to reset your spiritual pedometers back to zero today and launch afresh.

It's important to look *back*–burying regrets or dreams–and to look *ahead* in anticipation, but life can only be lived by looking *around* in the present moment. Wakeful people do that. They do something every day that's challenging, perhaps even transformative, for themselves and for all whom they meet along the road.

To wake up is to dwell in the "eternal now."

43
Ingratitude Can Produce Progress

*"Ingratitude is at the root of most or perhaps even all progress.
This was as true during the Stone Age as it is today."*
—P. J. WINGATE

Ingratitude as a way of life can be destructive. It breeds resignation, sometimes even despair. Yet, in creative doses, ingratitude can be catalytic for the good life. Our American heritage is filled with social reformers spurred to righteousness from a gnawing sense of ingratitude.

Dorothea Dix, Horace Mann, Clara Barton, Whitney Young, and others in our land were impelled to proclaim: "I can't, I won't abide conditions that contribute to the ills of my world!"

These humanitarians were ungrateful for anything that was injurious to the soul, body, and mind of their kin. For them gloom wasn't an option. They were bona fide agitators in the very practical sense that "they were the center pieces in the washing machine that gets the dirt out" (Jim Hightower).

Martin Luther King, Jr.'s phrase "creative maladjustment" denotes the same thing. Creative maladjustment keeps us morally sane, aesthetically sharp, and spiritually responsive creatures.

44
Explore the Bible Afresh

*"It ain't those parts of the Bible
that I can't understand
that bother me, but the parts
that I do understand."*
—MARK TWAIN

The best way to approach the Bible is through treating it as a criticizable friend: learn from each passage, even cherish some occasionally, but don't treat any as perfect, unflawed, and beyond reproach. Furthermore, as Twain intimates, when there are parts that unnerve you socially or vex you morally, be gutsy enough to accept their annoying relevance.

The Bible requires a reader who can sort out the deeper meanings underlying the intriguing myths. The Bible requires a reader who brings a high level of self-confidence and can declare: "This passage speaks to me," and "This one does not." The Bible requires a reader who will not be sidetracked by the inconsistencies and brutalities but can rise above them to uncover truths relevant to self-fulfillment and social responsibility.

There's the boy who opened his Bible at random to get advice on a difficult problem and had the misfortune to light on the words, "And Judas went and hanged himself." Not content with this cold comfort, he tried again, this time opening to the words, "Go and do likewise."

The Bible is not a level plateau but is comprised of mountain peaks and valleys, just like every other book. The prophecies of Amos scale the heights of justice for all peoples while Obadiah is filled with hatred for foreigners. It takes a discriminating, adult mind to live comfortably with such fierce disparities. The Bible, in all of its beauty and ugliness, is the product of human minds, many of them.

45
"Put the Big Rocks in First…"

An expert in time management was speaking to a group of college students. "Okay, it's time for a quiz," she announced as she pulled out a one-gallon mason jar and set it on the table. She also produced 12 fist-sized rocks and carefully placed them into the jar.

When the jar was filled to the top she asked, "Is the jar full?" Everyone in the class yelled, "Yes." Then she took out a bucket of sand and poured it into the jar, causing the sand to work itself down into the spaces between the big rocks. She asked again, "Is the jar full now?"

"Probably not," one of the crowd answered. Next the professor poured a pitcher of water into the jar until it was filled to the brim. Then she looked at the class and asked, "What's the point of this illustration?"

One student raised his hand and said: "The point is no matter how full your schedule is, if you really try hard you can always fit some more things in."

"No," replied the professor, "that's not what I had in mind. The truth this story teaches me is: 'If you don't put the big rocks in first, you'll never get them in at all.'"

Each of us selects our own big rocks: be they dreams, faith, relationships, education, or service. Remember to put them in first or you might later run out of room. Today, when you're reflecting upon this story, ask yourself these yoked questions: "What are the big rocks in my life? And am I putting them into the jar first?"

46
"We Can Never Be Born Enough."
—E. E. Cummings

We are born once. There is also being twice born. Mature spirituality goes further and claims that "we can never be born enough." Great human beings are not born the first time or even the second time. They edge toward degrees of near-greatness by their willingness to be born yet one more time. My friend, Phil Porter, calls this process "exformation," which transpires whenever we express ourselves outwardly through play, art, dance, sexuality, and other miscellaneous forms of embodiment.

Everyone is created once. Not every one is willing or able to undergo the necessary birthings thereafter. No surprise, because to be "created anew" can be painful, sometimes tormentingly so, as well as prove exhilarating.

47
Entertain Tips from the Golf Course

I don't play golf anymore, since I fractured my left elbow years back. Actually, I never was much of a golf enthusiast on the course anyway, but I do enjoy watching it: the blend of grace, torque, and pressure fascinate me. And there are life-lessons galore. Here are but three.

- First, play the ball where it lies.
- Second, the most crucial shot in golf is the one you're about to hit.
- Third, good golfers know how to get out of traps or trouble.

Can you point out other lessons from golf or a comparable activity of your liking?

48
Promote a Statue of Responsibility

"Freedom may degenerate into mere arbitrariness unless it is lived in terms of responsibleness. That is why I would recommend that the Statue of Liberty on the East Coast be supplemented by the Statue of Responsibility on the West Coast."
—VICKTOR FRANKL

Frankl was a psychotherapist who spent the bulk of his professional life—after surviving the horrors of a concentration camp during World War II—developing *logotherapy*, a health-approach centering upon the will to meaning. Frankl contended that the will to *mean-*

ing is ultimately a stronger force in our lives than Freud's will to *pleasure* or Adler's will to *power*, significant as they both are.

A portion of the meaningful life includes a commitment to responsible freedom. Freedom without responsibility leads to chaos. Responsibility without liberty ossifies into obligation. They need one another. Frankl's idea is astute. We would do well to have a "Statue of Responsibility on the West Coast" in order to provide moral balance in our country.

49
Bitterness Digs Two Graves

The fact is that bitterness never puts us in control but achieves the very opposite. It puts us in bondage to someone else and their perceived wrong by adding ours to the mix. We wind up imprisoned. There is no asset in being lugged around by anything or anyone else other than ourselves. But that's what animosity does.

Bitterness, after being sent forth, leaves an acrid and disagreeable taste in our mouth and heart as well. Bitterness is a diminishing emotion, because it digs two graves, yours and that of your target.

50
Grow Bolder As Older

"I speak truth, not as much as I would, but as much as I dare;
and I dare a little more as I grow older."
—MONTAIGNE (1533-1592)

Montaigne's *Essays* are soaking wet with timeless savvy. He knows that none of us speaks as much truthfulness as s/he might. It's understandable, even desirable, not to be totally honest (after all, open books only show two pages!), which might mean being a bit brutal.

I also appreciate Montaigne's confessing that he gambles more as he ages. I find that claim to be accurate as I amble down my homestretch. Elders have less to hide and fewer barriers to climb or reasons to fool anybody.

The Chinese word for *busy* is composed of two characters: heart *and* killing. This serves as a warning signal to be well-occupied but not burdened. We need to be enmeshed in ways that refrain from stifling the beat of our heart, let alone, killing it. The average human heart beats roughly 100,000 times a day; so the way to finish life well is to make each of those thumps amount to something.

51
Keep Your Loyalties Current

Virginia Woolf, somewhere in her anthology of brilliant writings, invites us to pursue "freedom from unreal loyalties." This is a crucial cleansing process often ignored by modern day clutterers. Few of us take the time to do spring cleaning in our homes, let alone roust out obsolete habits and extraneous commitments.

Our loyalties, to be real, must be current. I've found it productive to sit down and catalogue the places where I spend my time, energy, and money and rate which ones are up-to-date and which ones need to be shed. I am learning how to practice the art of relinquishment...surrendering things and tasks to the ether.

Spiritual pruning can be an arduous endeavor, since it entails letting go and mourning those things that are no longer vital for us. Once unburdened, we invariably feel relieved and en-lighten-ed.

52

Boredom Is an Equal Opportunity Unemployer

"Humans can endure to be ruined, torn from their friends, or overwhelmed with avalanches of misfortune, better than they can endure to be dull!"
—ANTHONY TROLLOPE

I'm reminded of a short story by William Saroyan entitled "The Man Whose Wife's Hair Was Too Long but Whose Understanding of Music Was Too Short." In this story, the husband is playing a cello and plays the same note over and over and over again. His wife, going out of her mind and not being able to stand it any longer, asks her husband plaintively. "Why, dear, do you play the same note over and over and over again? Other cellists play different notes."

To which her husband responded, "Balderdash. Other cellists play different notes, because they are trying to find the right one. I've already found mine!" Perhaps the right note, but one that's boring, utterly boring to the outside ear.

Inevitably we all face periodic patches of boredom; as they say, boredom is an equal opportunity unemployer. We all feel starched and stodgy sometimes, so let's make the most of this malaise. When we feel a dull spell coming on, inveigle using it as a sorting principle: a chance to realize that what you're doing isn't fulfilling. Stop the activity and move on to something more enjoyable. Bore in, bear down, go deeper, and explore broader.

Be willing to play an assortment of notes rather than staying stuck on one.

53
Aim High

"It is not a disgrace not to reach for the stars, but it is a disgrace to have no stars to reach for. Not failure, but low aim is our sin."
—Benjamin Mays

Aspiration literally means the capacity to breathe upwards. An aspirant is one who is willing to ascend or soar to meet a measured pursuit. They may not always reach it, but they confidently launch the quest.

A Harvard business professor declares that what regularly undermines an organization is not its problems (which are solvable) but its past successes that often breed a rigid identity, an unwillingness to grow. So each of us must ask: are we trapped by our previous accomplishments? What are we hanging on to that might inhibit forward movement or our continuing to breathe ahead?

54
Observe the Law of Boundaries

"You feed the patient not when s/he is crying that s/he is hungry but only when you feel the milk overflowing from your own nipples."
—Sheldon Kopp

There exists a basic guideline: the law of boundaries. In terms of evolution, plants and animals that selectively limited their growth survived, whereas the dinosaurs perished through excessive development.

The same principle applies in relationships. Our responses to the needs of other people must be selective, exemplify some hierarchy of priorities, lest we become overwhelmed. Whatever priorities for neighboring we produce, Jesus' germinal insight still holds: "Love thy neighbor as thyself." We can act compassionately only to the extent that we preserve our own integrity by loving ourselves.

When the Nazarene spoke of loving thy neighbor, he said, "as thyself." This means: to be effective in loving others we have to safeguard our own strength and well-being. A good, wise neighbor refrains from burning out or playing martyr.

55
Take Deep, Daily Bows

Awestruck, I wander among those enduring and endearing giants of Northern California, the Redwood trees.

I gaze beyond our Iowa acreage into a stunning, sunlit field of silent snow.

I behold the majestic, crashing surf of the Atlantic Ocean.

Without realizing it, after each of these moments, my hands merge and I make what the Zen Buddhists call *gasho*, and I take a bow, a deep bow.

A bow is not equivalent to blind adoration but refers to healthy surrender. A bow means paying respectful attention to all that arises in your trek. In bowing, we let our head drop, we hold our ego in check, and we open our heart. Taoism reminds us that in a storm, the bamboo tree that can bend and bow with the wind will survive. Hence, in my daily flow, I aspire to take four basic bows.

I bow to the needs and purposes of the universe.

I bow to the needs and purposes of the world community.

I bow to the needs and purposes of the humans I greet.

I bow to the needs and purposes of my own being.

You'd be surprised, as I've been, by the beneficial amount of bowing required during the course of an average day.

Gasho is gratitude in movement.

56
Absorb the Story of Brother Noah

There's the story of the minister who early in his career served in a river town ministry and had survived a sudden killer flood. Parson Smith had acted heroically, organizing folks and saving countless lives.

As we clergy are wont to do, the rest of Smith's ministry he kept on repeating the same grandiose story, embellishing it along the way. Upon arrival in Heaven, Reverend Smith was greeted by St. Peter who told him that the following night each newcomer would have a chance to introduce themselves and share a life-highlight.

"Oh great, oh wonderful, I can tell everybody about the incredible, mind-boggling Quincy flood!"

Peter said, "Yes, you can do so, but I need to alert you that Brother Noah will be in the gathered crowd tonight!"

Folks, each of our stories remains outstanding; yet there will always be someone in the gathered company who has experienced something perhaps grander than we have. So here's my counsel: tell your unique and dazzling story but offer it with as much grace and humility as possible. And the shorter, the better.

57
Engage in Creative Brooding

Mary, the mother of Jesus, was prone to brooding. She was known as one who sat on ideas and encounters, who "pondered things in her heart." Howard Thurman puts it similarly: "When you wake up on the morning, never rush out of bed, just simmer. And when you go to bed, never race to sleep, just simmer."

Whether you call it brooding or simmering, I encourage us to find our times and spots to sit quietly, to hover, and to hatch something by incubation, in the darkness.

We Westerners, who tend to be light addicts, must spend our entire lives growing a greater acquaintanceship with the demons and delights of darkness. Remember we were likely conceived in the dark nights of our parent's lovemaking and lived relatively contented lives for nine full months in utter darkness. The womb was dark but not fearful. We would do well to meditate upon our dark and silent origins and those of the cosmos itself.

Darkness furnishes an opportunity for inward, reflective time… a respite for creative brooding. What is it that you need to brood about or wrestle with in the quietude and darkness of your soul?

58
Hustle All the Way Home

"Whatsoever thy hand findeth to do,
do it with thy might."
—ECCLESIASTES 9:10

Charlie Brown is walking along with his sister, and Sally, looking at her report card, remarks, "what kind of a report card do you call this? I didn't even get any grades. All it says is 'Good Hustle.'"

Folks who are riveted on garnering certain letter grades often succumb to lethargy, caught either in the clutches of despair or cockiness. Well, when it's all said and done, Sally, I wouldn't mind getting a report card like yours. Hustle is the name of the game.

59
Be More than a Bystander

Too many folks decide to be like the man who said that he was "a Jehovah's Bystander." He yearned to be a Jehovah's Witness, but he didn't like to get involved. Yes, a true witness is someone who not only beholds what is going on, but, when called upon either by inner urge or outer need, is willing to get embroiled. Being spectators on the sidelines, lounging in front of TV or video screens, has become an all too frequent endeavor for young and old alike.

"Facebook" connections are important, but they pale next to greeting another person face-to-face. Our world is loaded with bystanders, those who loll about…living just this side of engagement.

They say that children remember 20% of what they hear, 30% of what they see, 50% of what they see and hear, 70% of what they say, and 90% of what they do. This isn't startling data, because the figures run pretty much the same for adults.

A creative, compassionate, courageous world demands more of its inhabitants than being bystanders.

60
"When I Haven't Any Blue, I Use Red."
—PABLO PICASSO

Often we find ourselves stuck in a dither of self-pity, because we don't have at our disposal a certain color or particular possibility. When we don't have blue, instead of halting operations, Picasso encourages us to use the other available options: red, green, yellow, lavender, and more.

A monochromatic life is enervating. We need to utilize with confidence a wide range of existent resources. What we have on hand invariably proves more interesting than we could ever imagine.

Ours can be an exquisitely colorful world, if we would employ our multi-hued palette.

61
Answer Your Special Call

When I was young, I said to God, 'Tell me the mystery of the universe.' But God answered, "That knowledge is reserved for me alone." So I said, "God tell me the mystery of the peanut." Then God said, "Well, okay, George, that's more nearly your size." And he told me.

The George in question was George Washington Carver, the scientist who developed hundreds of useful products from the peanut. Carver could have kept pining after impossible dreams, thus failing to do anything but fantasy-work. Instead, he discovered a soul-sized challenge, a duty that brought him joy, a call that Carver alone could answer. He settled for fathoming the mystery of the peanut rather than the inscrutable mystery of the universe. Horace Bushnell, the great New England preacher, used to say: "Somewhere under the stars God has a job for you to do, and nobody else can do it." Yes, a job with your name on it.

No matter if it takes countless trials and errors, keep plugging away until you find the call that matches your inner yearnings and the outer cries of the world.

One of comedienne Lily Tomlin's bizarre characters gets right to the nubbins of the matter: "When I was growing up, I always wanted to be somebody. Now I realize I should have been more specific."

Are you becoming increasingly specific in your personal and professional pursuits?

62
"Caring Is Everything!"

"In the sense in which we can ever be said to be at home in the world, we are at home not through dominating or explaining or appreciating but through caring and being cared for."
—MILTON MAYEROFF

When Baron von Hugel, the great philosopher and mystic, was dying, his niece bent over her uncle because she could see his lips moving and couldn't catch what he said. She put her ear close against his mouth and heard this, the last words that great saint ever uttered: "Caring is everything; nothing matters but caring!"

So it does: when skeptical, to care; when joyful, to care; when beleaguered, to care; and when angry, to care.

The notion of caring is dramatically conveyed in a story of a

---

little boy who begged a minister to come see his sister who was ill. The girl was 15; her mother had died and her father had abandoned the family, leaving her to care for her younger brothers and sisters. She had worked her fingers to the bone in providing for them, and now she was dying of pneumonia. The girl seemed to sense her imminent death and asked the minister, "Will I go to heaven?" He replied, "Of course you will, my dear." Then she said, "How will God know I belong; I haven't lived long enough to have done much?"

The minister paused a moment, then replied, "Show your hands, show God your hands!"

63
Don't Be Lukewarm

"I know thy works, that thou art neither cold nor hot, so because thou art lukewarm, I will spew thee out of my mouth."
—THE BOOK OF REVELATION

Communities, families, and congregations need their members to take stands, to risk yeses and nos, and to come clean in their commitments. Nothing's more frustrating than obsessive fence-sitting, incessant wobbling, being lukewarm of opinion or conviction, muddled in maybes.

Life is a partisan struggle. This doesn't mean that when we stake ourselves, we're absolutely certain or secure. We must act in good faith and with good will, even when complete evidence isn't forthcoming.

Wishy-washy politicians are suspect. Vacillating ethicists are too. There will be times when we're unsure, caught somewhere between partiality and impartiality, but that's no platform upon which to get elected. We should elect people for their convictions not their be-fuddlement.

Lukewarm people are about as appealing as tepid milk.

64
Consider Chanting

I'm a zealous singer, crooning most all the time, alone or accom-panied, but I've also grown a passion for chanting. Why? First off, whereas songs are tougher to memorize, chants are short, easy to recall in their entirety. Second, chants are so repetitive that they bring a deeper, almost hypnotic sense of serenity to my soul. The one drawback: don't chant while driving a car; it can provide a worse distractive danger than using a cell phone.

Did you know that the Benedictine monks can go for years on no more than 3 hours sleep per night provided they chant 6-8 hours every day?

65
We Are Known by Our Wounds

"Wounds and scars are the stuff of character. The word character means at root, 'marked or etched with sharp lines,' like initiation cuts."
—JAMES HILLMAN

I grew up feeling that in order to gain some character, I had to be pure and crisp, the "golden boy"...well-nigh perfect. Needless to say, it put a considerable crimp in my life. Only in my elder years have I recognized that it's all the nicks and bruises I've incurred or delivered that have cultivated my authentic character. All the rest has been my trying to impress the world rather than sculpt a thicker identity. I've finally made peace with my being vulnerable rather than my being impregnable.

In one of Alan Paton's South African novels, a character said of going to heaven, "When I go up there, which is my intention, the Big Judge will say to us, 'Where are your wounds?' and, if I haven't any, God will say, 'Was there nothing to fight for?' I couldn't face that question," concludes Paton's character.

We are known by our wounds, be they emotional, physical, intellectual, or spiritual. We don't need to get enmeshed in scar-swap meets where everyone tries to out-swagger the next person. Nonetheless, our scraps and scrapes are leading indicators of what we've loved and where we've struggled, and allude to the battles we've endured or should have avoided.

Each of us, before he or she is finished on earth, needs to ask and answer: "For whom am I willing to go to the barricades? For what, if anything, would I give up my very breath? Who am I when no one's around to evaluate my behavior?"

66
"Be of Good Cheer!"

"I tried in my time to be a philosopher,
but cheerfulness was always breaking in."
—SAMUEL JOHNSON

Being a philosopher literally means to be a "lover of wisdom." There's no reason why such a pursuit shouldn't include humor and lots of it. Unfortunately, our society has tended to equate philosophy, theology, and the sciences as being domains of the serious, even ponderous, rather than the playful.

Whether you are a philosopher, politician, or plumber, whatever your vocation might be, may you be available for any and all cheerfulness waiting to break through. There is little worse than being caught up in a grinding job. We tend to quit jumping around much as adults, but this is a grievous mistake; for flapping and bounding about, either in frustration or joy, is a strong gauge of our aliveness.

However, remember that Jesus invited us to "be of good cheer," shunning the shallower Aramaic equivalent of "cheerio."

67
"A Garden Is a Lovesome Thing."
—T. W. Browne

"Lovesome" is a quaint word that combines winsome and lovely, which is precisely what a garden can be if it receives sufficient care and nutrients. A garden is a thing of beauty and a job forever.

According to Genesis, tilling the garden was the original task and one that we would need to honor all the way home. In fact, the Hebrew word for *till* carries the connotation of serving, not just digging and plowing. And isn't the word *tender* in all of its various meanings just right to describe the nature of our kinship with the earth?

We need to tend our own little patches. And more. We need to be concerned about the quality of our universal garden, the entire ecosystem. What we were invited to do in Eden, we're challenged to do upon waking up every morn.

68

Be Concerned about Every Last Child

In the Masai warrior culture, the inevitable daily greeting, adult to adult, is: "And how are the children of the village?" signaling that the barometer of a society's well-being is how its younger ones are being treated and doing. Are they being fed properly, cared for regularly, and given hope for shaping beautiful and just tomorrows? I will never forget visiting a teenager who had been abused and was living in a "safe center" for women and children. Above the door as one entered the house were found these words: "Remember, children are meant to be heard and listened to and believed!"

Jesus was considered an unconventional social revolutionary precisely because he allowed children and women to accompany him in public and because he treated them not as outcasts or chattel but as full-fledged companions in life's journey. In ancient society, as well as today's world, children have never been granted social equality, although their oppression is often disguised beneath layers of guilt-driven goodies and sweet-hearted rhetoric. The staggering fact is that the average time we adults spend shopping per week is six hours and the average time we spend playing with our own children is forty minutes. And things are getting worse: the reduced time parents spend with their offspring today compared to 1965: 40%.

If there's one unmistakable truth resident in the oft-bewildering, shadowy ministry of the Galilean rabbi, it was his unfailing push for a better status for the marginalized of society, especially the lost, the powerless, and the children.

We would do well to heed his literal exhortation to "let the children come up to me and do not try to stop them," recorded in Mark, Matthew, and Luke. And I'm not just referring to our own children but also to our being equally concerned about earth's other children: children we will never know personally, children from foreign lands, children who stagger and reel on life's edges, and children not yet born.

Geoffrey Canada, Harlem activist-educator, challenges any of us who are desirous of reviving civilization, one step at a time, one person at a time: "You never know what will save or lose a child, so save the child close to you." And if you can't really *save* them, at least be willing to *serve* them.

69
Be a Full-blown Chooser

"Choose ye this day whom ye will serve."
—JOSHUA 24:15

This Hebraic passage reminds us that our goals must be selected anew daily. It isn't enough to decide every three years or even every three months what is precious enough to follow. We need daily reinforcement. We must be intentional when we arise every morn. Each new day summons us to be thoughtful and generous servants but neither slaves nor saviors.

The word *decision* is akin to choosing and comes from the Latin term for "cutting off." To make the right choice is to eschew wrong ones. To decide for *this* rather than *that* means to cut off *that* so that *this* might be affirmed positively. Human life resembles a necessary surgical operation where we're obliged to suffer the cutting out of this part in order to secure the proper function of the total organism.

We're called to be decision-makers not defaulters. Sometimes we need to exhibit the daring courage of a pioneer, staking ourselves in a foreign or difficult territory. If we can just manage a

---

beginning move, the rest will follow.

John F. Kennedy loved to tell the story of how as a boy, he and his friends would hike in the countryside and when they came to an orchard wall that seemed too doubtful to scale and too difficult to permit their voyage to continue, they took off their hats and tossed them over the wall. Then they had no choice but to follow them.

So may it be with us. May we prove intrepid enough to throw some hats over some walls and then track them down.

70
Learn to Fuss Effectively

"A country can be flawed as a marriage or family or person is flawed, but 'love it or leave it' is a coward's slogan. There's more honor in 'love it and get it right. Love it, love it and never shut up.'"
—Barbara Kingsolver

Privately and publicly, don't settle for the status quo. Keep fussing over the flaws in all your loves, then labor to improve some of them. Fiddling, fuming, feuding, and fussing are integral to any vital encounter in your life. I'll never forget an elder in my Iowa congregation who said the following: "I was born a WASP, a condition I won't ever be able to change, but a condition I'll keep working on my entire life to improve!"

And here's a related tip to heed from the Recovery Movement: start by putting your body in the right place and your mind will eventually follow.

Obtain a Letter of Reference from the Poor

"Nobody gets into heaven without a letter of reference from the poor."
—ANNE LAMOTT

Years ago, the city of Toledo had a mayor called "Golden Rule Jones." Once in a while he went down to preside at police court. On a winter day, during the depression of the 1930s, the police brought in a man charged with stealing groceries. The man pleaded guilty and offered no excuses except that he had no money and had no job.

"I've got to fine you," said the mayor. "You stole, not from the community responsible for these conditions but from a particular person. So I will fine you ten dollars." Then the mayor reached into his pocket, pulled out a bill, and said, "Here's the money to pay your fine."

Then he picked up his hat and handed it to the bailiff. "Now I'm going to fine everybody in this courtroom fifty cents or as much thereof as they happen to have with them for living in a town where a person has to steal groceries in order to eat. Bailiff, go through the courtroom please and collect the fines and give them to the defendant." The mayor knew that the material needs of other folks are the spiritual needs of everyone.

We all shoulder the economic responsibility not merely for ourselves and our family but also for the weakest and most exploited members of our larger community. For, "to whom much is given, much will be required." Whenever we spend time working with homeless folks, we are putting a name and face on the poor. We are being the humans we were put on earth to be.

There's a relevant South American blessing: "For those who are hungry, give them bread and for those who have bread, give them a hunger for justice." In either case, we stand in need of one another's assistance and service. We are creatures joined at the heart and hip.

72
Sometimes Just Clap and Cheer

Suzie was trying out for a part in the school play. Her mother knew she wanted one but was afraid she might not be chosen. You know how nervous we parents can be when "our egos" are on the line. Well, parts were given out, and Suzie rushed into her mother's arms, bursting with pride and excitement. "Mom, guess what? I've been chosen to clap and cheer!"

I imagine the mother was angling for a more substantial, glorious role for her precious daughter. Understandably so, for our well-being as parents is often directly reflected in the success of our children. But sometimes our offspring are satisfied with just being involved in dramatic shows. They're pleased with being called to "clap and cheer."

Come to think of it, that's not an insignificant or unworthy role for most adults most of the time. It sure beats sitting on the sidelines: gawking or moaning.

73
Die Climbing

"The traditional Taoist maxim–'Heaven, Earth, Humanity'–places the importance of heaven and earth before that of humanity, reminding us that we are only a part of everything under the sky and on the earth."
—DANNY SWICEGOOD

I resonate with Jacob's ladder, which is prudently placed midway between heaven and earth, so that Jacob and the rest of humanity can be seen climbing back and forth, forth and back between soil and sky, the imminent and the transcendent. The key to a fulfilling existence is never to rest secure or cease our climbing.

At Chamonix, on a stone that marks the grave of a guide who perished ascending the Alps, are written these three suggestive words: "He died climbing!"

We will stumble and fall, from dawn to dusk; that's a certainty. No one climbs unimpeded and uninterrupted through life. We're constantly derailed; so let's quit trying to be comfortable all the time. But after any and every fall, the question persists: Do we get up and keep plugging? Do we keep on climbing, yea "die climbing?"

74
Employ Your Two Hearts

"Great people have two hearts; one bleeds and the other forebears."
—KAHLIL GIBRAN

We need two hearts and would use them as interchangeably as we employ our right and left feet. When friends are ill, they desire us to weep with them amidst fear and agony. They also covet individuals who can step aside from the turmoil and remain sturdy as rocks. But there's a fine line, isn't there? If our heart turns maudlin and syrupy, then we can quickly sentimentalize into irrelevance. On the other hand, if our heart stands faint and detached, it's liable to harden in no time at all–a ruinous result for everyone concerned.

Our task is to keep both hearts ready, on call, for service to our kin, then to know which to use and when.

75

Pain Is a Potential Ally

*"One of our great assets is our pain.
It is a bridge to the pain of our neighbor."*
—B. J. CANNON

Pain isn't necessarily a growth experience. It can drive us crazy, to an early grave, or at least to a life of anguish. As humorist George Burns bemoaned: "Hey, I wish I could get over my arthritis. I've had it forever, at least ever since it first came out!"

Some people succumb to modest pain. Others endure a barrage. What makes the difference between victims and endurers in the struggle with inevitable pain? Well, one factor is our willingness to confront pain, staring, even screaming at it, just befriending our pain whenever possible. Facing pain doesn't mean sitting on an avoidable cactus, but it can mean daring sometimes to grab the nettle.

If we don't ignore our sorrow, if we don't waste our pain, if we don't wallow in self-pity, and if we are responsive to the thorny wisdoms available in our calamities, we'll not only make it through to the other side, we may even emerge stronger.

Additionally, when we visit others in their sorrow or hurt, it lightens the load of both of us. It builds a potential bridge, not always but often.

76
Keep Sailing On

"The known is finite, the unknown infinite; intellectually we stand on an islet in the midst of an illimitable ocean. Our business in every generation is to reclaim a little more land."
—T. H. Huxley

The first Europeans to land in the Americas were actually adventurers from Norway, Iceland, or Greenland in the late tenth and early eleventh centuries. They certainly settled briefly in Newfoundland and may have landed elsewhere on the Atlantic coast of North America.

Nonetheless, Columbus's expedition was distinguished for being the first recorded European expedition to cross the Atlantic Ocean in warm or temperate latitudes. It entailed much longer ocean passages than previously undertaken.

Like Columbus, we don't all make initial discoveries. Most of us will uncover little, if anything, very original during our lifetimes. Our gifts resemble those of Columbus. We bring something special to what already exists. We make the same voyages as our predecessors but in our own fashion.

Columbus was a flawed individual. His inflexibility combined with piety and opportunism produced behavior not far from paranoia. He was also petty, as when he claimed for himself the prize money he had promised to the first crew member to sight westward land.

And yet, despite all his imperfections and failings, all you really have to remember is that Columbus wrote in the log of his first voyage across the uncharted Atlantic: "This day we sailed on..."

77

Reach Out in Solidarity

I resonate with the Blackfoot tribe in the manner in which they greet one another. They don't start with "how are you?" but rather "how are the connections?" implying that the core of life consists of bonds. Life ultimately has to do with how we function *with* rather than *apart* from or *against* one another in the world.

There are those who reach *up* in deference, reach *back* in nostalgia, or reach *down* in patronizing. Collaborators are those who reach *out* in solidarity. Strong leaders know how to do that. They are neither jealous nor frightened to divide the burden and multiple the glory. They create institutions that resemble the jazz combo as a harmonious, mutually supportive, and creative alliance of soloists.

Paul, in the Christian scriptures, invites people to address one another as "yokefellows." He urges us to treat one another in a truly collaborative fashion. We are solitary creatures, to be sure, but change the *t* to a *d*, and we are also solidary beings. We are yokefellows.

Here's an illustration. A girl and her mother were walking along the road when they came across a large stone. The girl said to her mother, "Do you think if I use all my strength, Mom, I can move this rock?" The mother answered, "Yes, dear, if you use all your power, I'm sure you can do it."

The girl began to push the rock. Exerting herself as much as she could, the youngster pushed and pushed. The rock didn't move. Discouraged, she said to her Mother, "You were wrong, I can't do it." Her mom placed an arm around her daughter's shoulder and tearfully said, "No, my daughter. You didn't use all your strength; you didn't ask *me* to help!"

78
Get Committed

You probably know the yarn about the chicken and the pig who were looking over the fence at a huge billboard picturing a plate of ham and eggs. "They couldn't do it without us," said the chicken. "Doesn't it make you feel great to think you're part of all that?" "Well," said the pig, "you've got to consider that for you it's just a contribution, while for me it's a total commitment!"

Families, partnerships, and communities cannot remain healthy or vital on mere contributions, tokens of record, now and again. Our society has gone through a period of antipathy to qualities such as duty, obligation, and sacrifice. Current commentators believe we're returning to an ethic of commitment among the younger generation. I hope they're right.

We need more people willing to plumb the depths of relationship before hurrying on to yet another liaison. We need individuals who seek "solids" rather than "highs" in their daily lives. Intentional tribes need people who hang tough, weather storms, resolve conflicts rather than threaten departure when their egos are barely bruised.

Life demands staying power or commitment, literally where we "send ourselves with." Here's an illustration. Fritz Kreisler had just finished a concert and was going backstage when an enthusiastic music fan cried out: "Mr. Kreisler, I'd give my life to play as you do!" Quietly, yet fervently, the master musician replied, "Madam, I did, I did!"

79

Play Hard, Play Fair, and Nobody Hurt (If Possible)!

"The surest way to remain a winner is to win once, and then not to play any more."
—Ashleigh Brilliant

There is definitely a place for competition: that fierce yet friendly combat at the bridge table or on the tennis court and rugby field. Believe me, I'm a tenacious competitor; when I play, I play to perform well—yea, to win.

Yet there are other ways to play too. In infinity volleyball, for example, the object is to see how long the ball can be kept in the air. Just as in regular volleyball, each team must hit the ball no more than three times before sending it over the net. Both teams count the number of times the ball has been hit, and both share the final score. The rules for infinity volleyball and other such play-fair games are basic: play hard, play fair, and nobody hurt (if possible)!

An American father and his twelve-year-old daughter were enjoying a beautiful Saturday in Hyde Park, London, and playing catch with a Frisbee. Few in England had seen a Frisbee in 1964, and a small group of strollers gathered to watch this strange sport. Finally, one Britisher went over to the father: "Sorry, to bother you, I've been watching you for a quarter of an hour. Who's winning?"

People throughout the globe seem dead set on victory, don't we? But being competitive doesn't mean having to be combative. You can be a contender without turning contentious. The truth is that, in important attachments, winning isn't paramount, satisfaction is. Ultimately we're here on earth to play *with*, not *against*, one another. Plus, it's more fun that way!

80
Be a Comforter

"One day Joshu fell down and called out, 'Help me up! Help me up!' A monk came and lay down beside him. Joshu got up and went away."
—ZEN STORY

The monk didn't try to save Joshu; he suffered alongside him. The monk did what was necessary: nothing more and nothing less. He joined Joshu for awhile, and that act of support was sufficient. Joshu proceeded to lift himself up, inspired and braced by the monk's company, however brief.

The word "comfort" literally means placing our strength next to the weakness of another person, sometimes actually lying down beside her or him...for however long it might take for restoration of either body or soul.

Being a comforter is a high and holy calling.

81
Life Is 100 Times More Complicated

"Remember all those things we used to blame on the devil and all those things we left up to god? Now it all seems 100 times more complicated."
—JOSEPH PINTAURO

It's tempting to toss all our dilemmas onto some external source by saying: "the devil made me do it" or the government, my mother, Wall Street, my boss, or my mate. The truth is that it's unfair and pointless to blame much of anything on realities outside yourself. It renders them omnipotent and leaves you helpless. Sooner or later we must realize our collusion or culpability in our own crises and make the appropriate changes.

Banking on god isn't much more helpful than dumping on the devil. Surely there are moments to seek transcendent strength, guidance, and companionship. We are interdependent with all that is. Yet, finally, we can't let George or Gertrude or the goddess lead our own life. We must do it or it doesn't get done. As my friend says: "If it is to be, it is up to me!"

Try running for governor of yourself.

82
Conduct Trumps All

A child brought home her school report card with satisfactory grades in everything except conduct. When the father queried her, the child answered, "Well, Dad, conduct is my most difficult subject!"

Her sensibility actually holds true for young people and adults as well. Our conscience can be keen and our character outstanding on paper; but conduct is how we actually shape our lives out in the open. When we are with other folks, we need to rightly ask: Does my own conduct raise others to a level of greater or lesser justice, love, and mercy?

Conduct will always remain the most demanding class in the curriculum of life.

83
Pick Your Spots to be *Punny*

Some say the pun is the lowest form of humor. Others claim it requires erudition and alacrity. In any case, I've found puns to be humor at its most democratic, because their usage is employed by any and all who would risk novel, spontaneous twists of conversation.

A pair of punny examples. Much has been written about helping plants to grow by playing music or singing to them. Success has now been reported by a person who has been experimenting with obscene "fern" calls.

At a local popular racket club, you have to book well ahead if you want to reserve a tennis court. One enthusiast was so concerned about not losing her booking that she left early from her husband's funeral. It was a case of putting the "court before the hearse!"

84
Cope with Conflict

*"Conflict by definition means only this: we need to change our
way of dealing with each other; the old way no longer works.
Conflict is a neutral term, neither positive nor negative."*
—COLMAN MCCARTHY

There are several salient things to note about conflict.

- On earth, this third-rate planet revolving around a second-rate sun, we are riddled with conflict. The only question is whether or not we will resolve each clash in a creative and constructive manner.

- Beware of and avoid sure-fire conflict escalators such as changing the topic, dwelling only in the past, pushing another's buttons, and going passive.
- Don't *flee* and don't *fight*, rather *face* one another and work to create a third acceptable reality. Facing means staying at the table. Remember the Last Supper scene with Jesus and the 12 disciples. Jesus breaks bread, passes a cup, and says: "Someone here will betray me." That's a pretty frightening sentiment to risk at such a time of fellowship, but it ends up being a painful truth, for Jesus was betrayed by both Peter and Judas before his career was over. Even so, and here's my point, Jesus didn't flee or fight. He didn't leave the table.
- If you want to create a safe space for people in conflict, get them to do something together rather than merely quibble. Rearrange furniture, create a drawing, take a walk, plant trees…together.

In conflict management we need what someone has called GRIT–"graduated reciprocal reduction in tension." Each side needs to give not *in,* but *toward,* some imaginative result.

85
Attend to the Little Things

"Little things console us because little things afflict us."
—BLAISE PASCAL

Unheralded deeds and humdrum decisions cannot be underestimated in life. Lots of us ignore little things and wait around for splashy events. But it's customarily the little things that make or break our days.

Cartoonist Jules Feiffer talked about the "little murders" that gnaw away at our loves. Indeed, it is the petty irritations that erode our friendships. Conversely, it's also the modest moves that nourish lives, moment by moment.

A friend of mine says that before he can contemplate dating again, his "recovery" program has challenged him to relate without clinging and being over-expectant, first with a rock (he's already nicknamed a special rock in the yard "carpe" from *carpe diem*), then plans are underway to move on to obtain a kitten, then perhaps...a person. But Peter's certainly in no rush.

Little things can both rattle and console us.

"Long looking" means calming down and taking our spiritual pulse. If you don't believe me, follow the advice of the baseball wit Yogi Berra, who declared: "Hey, you can see a lot by watching!"

86

Be Congruent

Someone once charged David Hume, the agnostic, with being inconsistent because he went to hear the orthodox Scottish minister John Brown preach sometimes on Sundays. Hume replied, "I don't believe all that he says, but he does. And once a week I like to hear a person who believes what they say!" That's precisely the challenge for all of us: to say and do what we believe. We're called to be congruent...mind and spirit, words and actions.

John Haynes Holmes, one of the premier early-20th-century activist ministers in America, was once explaining to his colleague Robert Collyer the objectives of socialism. Holmes hoped that through socialism people might be aided according to their needs

---

and rewarded according to their abilities.

There was a long pause. Collyer shook his head and said, "I don't fully understand it, John. And what I understand, I don't like." Then he smiled, and said, "But if you like it and believe in it, then go ahead and promote it for all you're worth."

May our inner and outer beings match up, grow in alignment. May we preach and practice for all we're worth, every last one of us.

87

Switch on Your Inner Light

"Let your steps be guided by such light as you have."
—St. Paul

None of us possesses all the light we truly need: light as spark, light as truth, and light as warmth. Nonetheless, we each boast a measure of light in our souls. Instead of waiting around for magical bursts of light from beyond, let's employ the power that is already within. We have untapped capacity to brighten our days, radiate energy and glow, and guide our very life-steps.

"This little light of mine, I'm going to let it shine" runs the spiritual. We may be pleasantly startled when we turn on our inner lights.

88

Feed and Care for Your Conscience

"I will not cut my conscience to fit the fashions of our time."
—LILLIAN HELLMAN

Lillian Hellman (1905-1984) was a controversial political play-wright who was blacklisted for her leftist activities in the 1950s. Hellman's income drastically dwindled, and she had to sell her family farm. Called before the House Un-American Activities Committee (HUAC), Hellman refused to reveal the names of Communist theater friends. Upon her death she resolutely stood by her conscience yet again, establishing two funds: one for progressive arts and sciences, the other to further her chosen radical causes.

Our conscience shrinks or enlarges, depending on the particular concern, but its importance in our lives endures. The way to refine our conscience is from internal nudging more than external bludgeoning. I find it useful, periodically, to accomplish what I call an "inner housecleaning," an activity that entails delving into my mind and heart and throwing out worn-out thoughts or deplorable attitudes, anything that blocks me from being a better and bolder human being.

I resonate with the words of activist minister Stephen Fritchman:

Today's surgeons can transplant hearts, kidneys, and other human organs; but no man or woman in the health sciences can yet transplant a conscience. Feed and care for your conscience as you do your brain; neither can be replaced.

Consistency Is a Hobgoblin

There's certainly some virtue in consistency. I heard of the judge who asked a man his age. He replied, "Thirty!" The judge said, "You've given that age in this court for the last five years." The man replied, "Yes, I know, but I'm not one of those who says one thing today and another thing tomorrow."

On the whole, consistency is overrated as a virtue. First off, it's only valuable if we're doing the right things. Furthermore, to maintain a record of absolute consistency in all we say or do is not only impossible, but often undesirable. Who wants to hook up with a robot?

As parents, partners, and professionals we're pressured by society to become predictable. We've made a hobgoblin of consistency, to use Emerson's felicitous phrase. Life is filled with ambiguities, and our task is to live kindly and smartly in the chaotic midst of those inconsistencies.

There's merit to what Oscar Wilde said: "Consistency is the last refuge of the unimaginative." We need to leap out of ruts, savor life, and vary our agendas. Instead of rising at 6:05, why not try getting up at 5:06?

Finally, inconsistency is often necessitated by changes that are grounded in moral growth. Gandhi was asked why he could so easily contradict this week what he had said just last week. He replied that it was because this week he knew better.

90
"The Character of a Person Is Known from Their Conversations."
—Menander, Greek Dramatist

Heidegger, interpreting Holderlin, says that to be human is to be a conversation, a strange yet striking way of claiming that communion is the basis of living humanly. A conversation literally means "turning with or toward" another person.

Psychoanalyst Karen Horney enumerated three basic patterns of emotional movement: turning *against* or aggression, turning *away* or retreat, and turning *toward* or dialogue. There are times when we need to withdraw. Perhaps, in self-defense, we will occasionally be driven to choose combat. However, the healthiest form of "living humanly" is conversation or engagement.

The Russian composer Igor Stravinsky said that after he and Aldous Huxley became good friends, he gave away all his encyclopedias and just asked Huxley whatever he wanted to know, then got absorbed in full-bore conversation.

That's a bit extreme for my tastes, since every house should own a set of reliable reference books or have ready access to a library or on-line references; nonetheless, Stravinsky clearly believed, and so do I, that vital conversations generated by bright and sensitive humans trump inert volumes and social media instruments every time.

Blessed Are the Meek

"We are very blessed that it is the meek who are to inherit the earth,
for they can be trusted with it."
—MADELEINE L'ENGLE

We link the words "meek" and "little," but true meekness is neither small nor weak. And meek isn't equivalent to sad resignation. Rather it refers to a gentleness that is graced with sinew. The meek aren't harsh or covetous. They don't trample in brute force but rather navigate life in a reverential manner. Others claim only their rights, but the meek are concerned about their duties.

In a world where human life is threatened, genuine meekness becomes our final hope. With meekness comes an astonishing reward: inheritance of the earth. It comes as gift and legacy. It comes because the meek would neither seize nor squander it.

"Courage Is the Primary Virtue."

"Life shrinks or expands in proportion to one's courage."
—ANAIS NIN

I hold courage to be the primary virtue, as Ben Jonson claimed. Why? Because without emotional, intellectual, or spiritual bravery we don't even entertain, let alone activate, the other virtues, such as love and justice. Courage gets us unstuck and moving.

Often you and I want to wait for all the evidence to arrive, be-

---

fore we risk something. And we're logjammed, because we keep waiting for conclusive evidence to appear. But, alas, we never know enough.

Rabbi Rami Shapiro was asked if he could whisper only two words to a dying person, what would he mouth? He replied: "Courage and love." You know what? I'd whisper the same two words to a newborn as well: "Courage and love."

So, go ahead, take a risk, show courage, and stick out your neck! Then, as your confidence mounts, consider making bravery one of your routine practices.

93
Resolve to Be Useful

"Formerly he was useless to you, but now
he is indeed useful [onesimus] to you and me."
—PHILEMON, V. 11

This tiny little book of the Bible is commonly skipped over. After all, it's only three-fourths of a page long, nestled between Titus and Hebrews. Briefly, it tells the story of Paul, while in prison, meeting a runaway named Onesimus whom he befriends. Paul feels so strongly about Onesimus turning his life around that he becomes an enthusiastic advocate in assisting him out of confinement.

Paul makes a telling remark about Onesimus, a remark relevant to all of us. He states that Onesimus was formerly useless but now that he's found himself, he can become useful. Note that the very name Onesimus in Greek means "useful." Therefore, when he became true to his real being and purpose in life, Onesimus genuinely became useful.

Same for us. When we chase not someone else's identity but

fulfill our own, then, and only then, are we valuable contributors to society. In answer to the question, "What do you want to be?" a third-grader wrote: "I would like to be myself. I tried to be other things, but I always failed."

Rings true, doesn't it?

94
Negotiate Covenants

Several years ago, my life-mate, Carolyn, and I came upon the notion that when each of our six grandchildren reached the age of 10, we would mount a special week-long trip to a destination of mutual choice. This would furnish precious one-on-one, in-depth, time together, just the three of us. When Corinne turned 10, our sights settled on a tropical rainforest eco-adventure to the jungles of Costa Rica.

Of the three of us, I'm clearly the least bold. I admit to being fearful of turbulent waters and lofty altitudes. Nonetheless, we went tubing in the raging river (where I capsized twice, thoroughly bruising my body on boulders, as well as losing my helmet) and zip-lining (the very next day) at speeds up to 35 miles per hour, while soaring 650 feet above a jungle loaded with wild beasts. Such antics hardly constitute my idea of fun. There was one reason, and one reason alone, why I risked these "harebrained" escapades: Corinne Chapman, our granddaughter.

Corinne and I negotiated a covenant, which, in retrospect, turned out to be a trip highlight, certainly for me—a deal that would produce life lessons for our respective futures. The nubbins of the covenant was expressed thusly:

"Okay, let's make a vow, Corinne: I will shake hands with two dragons this week—tubing and zip-lining—to the best of my ability and nerves, if you will promise to face your own upcoming fears (be they physical or emotional, relational or professional) in life. Okay?"

Corinne and I shook hands and hugged, agreeing to muster mutual bravery in the facing of our body and soul fears, starting then and there, in the jungles of Costa Rica.

95

Deliver CPR

"Compassion is where peace and justice kiss."
—PSALMIST

Clearly, we can't be all things to all people; plus a condition exists called compassion-fatigue wherein we give so much to others that we feel depleted and sulky. Nonetheless, there are those moments and exchanges every day where we're summoned to deliver CPR (the "compassionate person's response"), to serve, where needed, with joy…nourishing both giver and receiver.

The Greek verb *splangchnizomai* is an expression in the gospels that appears only twelve times and is exclusively used in reference to Jesus or God. It means "to be moved with compassion." The *splangchna* are the entrails of the body, or as we might say today, the guts. They are the place where our most intimate and intense emotions are located: anguishing, rejoicing, and raging.

When the Christian scriptures speak about Jesus' compassion as his being moved in the entrails, they're expressing something quite deep and mysterious, rather than conveying superficial sympathy. Are you and I willing to go straightway to the entrails, to the guts? Are we willing to be fully compassionate people?

Study the Wisdom of Divali

In the Western world we have a tendency toward dichotomies. You are either good or evil, nothing in between. The Hindus are subtler: everything in existence is a mixture of both; therefore their aim, although not necessarily their accomplishment, is to let the good predominate.

This is reflected in the marvelous myth of Narakarasura, on whose birthday Divali, the notable fall festival of India, is celebrated. In Indian lore, Narakarasura was an evil demon, but he was also the son of the great Preserver-god, Vishnu. Narakarasura was by no means all bad. He did much good in his life, and for a long while the good predominated.

However, he became an increasingly evil influence, and when the evil began to outweigh the good, Vishnu decreed that his son must die. "But," protested Narakarasura, "don't the scriptures say that good follows good as evil follows evil?" "Yes," said Vishnu, "that's correct."

"Then what do I get for the good I have done?" asked Narakarasura. "What do you think you should get?" asked Vishnu. "I think," said Narakarasura slyly, "that when you celebrate the triumph of good over evil, you should do it on my birthday!" That is why the festival of Divali falls on the birthday of an evil demon.

Divali reminds us that, in the long run, the best solution is to proclaim an armistice and welcome the warring factions into the human commonwealth. Opposites belong together; dualisms can be bridged; and the contradictions of life need to be encompassed or clasped in creative tension.

97
Copy Crabgrass

*"Faith is rooted in the will to live. It is like crabgrass. It will not give up.
Stone walls are no match for it. It can break through cement.
It defies poison and surgery. It is indomitable."*
—JOHN WOLF

We like to envision ourselves as being beautiful plants or flowering trees. But check it out: the most successful among our species are more like dandelions, weeds, crabgrass, aren't they? Why? Because they persevere. They possess creeping stems and sprout up when least expected and against all odds.

They keep coming back. There's a lot to be said for crabgrass!

98
"Few Things Are Needful..."

*"Few things are needful to make the wise happy but nothing satisfies the
fool; and this is the reason why so many of us are miserable."*
—FRANCOIS LA ROCHEFOUCAULD

Some folks are bottomless pits. They never seem to acquire enough emotional highs. They crave possessions or they collect spiritual experiences like pieces of jewelry. The truth is that our human needs are rather basic. Food, shelter, warmth, love, and significance are the fundamentals of the full life.

Most every religion warns its adherents against an overweening ego or a voracious appetite. In Buddhism *tanha,* or craving, is

---

the central cause of universal suffering. We become attached to people, possessions, power...and, yes, food and drink. Everything is reduced to me, my, and mine! We drown in our own "unquenchable thirst."

We reach a goal; then we crave yet another one, just beyond or around the corner. We fall in love with novelty. We settle into a meaningful relationship, then we crave fresher, better love...somewhere else.

The wisdom of Mark Nepo lands on target: "Having the life you want is being present to the life you have."

99

Be a Critic Not a Croaker

"Criticism should not be querulous and wasting, all knife and root-puller, but guiding, instructive, inspiring, a south wind, not an east wind."
—RALPH WALDO EMERSON

So much criticism is geared to knife another. It looks a lot like condemnation. Without compassion, without perspective, without humility, our criticism can often prove devastating.

The only point of criticism then is to guide, instruct, and inspire our brothers and sisters along life's precipices. A south wind enables someone to move forward, propelled by a favorable breeze. An east wind drives people sideways. And the way that criticism works best, from my own personal experience, is asking thus: "In what manner do you want your feedback? How can you best handle my criticism?"

But there's a fine line to walk between being a critic and a croaker. As Benjamin Franklin lamented: "There are croakers in every country, always boding its ruin."

Pessimists abound. Frightened, they rush to terrify others around them. We need critics but not croakers.

Critics, at their best, are willing to pinpoint flaws in those realities they cherish. They may complain but never for long. They perceive weaknesses and strengths, starting with their own. They don't augur ruin; they invite renovations. In fact, a useful critic never gripes without offering a constructive proposal.

Away with croakers and in with critics!

100
Discover Your Niche

"I want to be famous in the way a pulley is famous, or a buttonhole, not because it did anything spectacular, but because it never forgot what it could do."
—NAOMI SHIHAB NYE

Rarely does one land upon any shrewder counsel than that of the poet Naomi Shihab Nye. In essence she is urging her fellow humans—if we truly seek realization, let alone any measure of fame—zealously to become the best version imaginable of our singular selves. We need to remember, then embody, what it is that we do in our own inimitable fashion. Buttonholes don't aspire to be pulleys, and pulleys don't scramble to become rivers. Buttonholes consistently perform their proper function, and so do pulleys and rivers.

A niche is nothing more and nothing less that an especially suitable place or position. If each of us would strive to find our own peculiar niche in this wondrous universe, we may never accomplish anything spectacular but, in our ardent questing, we will discover the sole reason each and every one of us is roaming the earth.

101
"Everything We Consciously and Unconsciously Do Is Our Curriculum."
—Angus McLean

The word curriculum meant originally the course for a foot race held in the great amphitheaters of the world. The main human curriculum must never focus solely upon technology but on service, not on information but on wisdom, the deeper stuff of our odyssey.

The course around which our children, youth, adults, and societies travel centers upon raising and responding to the perennial queries of existence, such as: Who am I? Where did I come from? Where is my destination? Who will be my chosen companions? What truly sustains me? Am I essentially a fault-finder or a good-finder? Am I imperious or gracious in my dealings with strangers? How can I return love to the Love that created me and will not let me go or let me off? How can I stay in one place and still keep growing up and on?

Don't cram or overload your course work: it will suffice to tackle one question at a time.

102
Embrace Rather than Solve Mystery

"The most beautiful experience we can have is the mysterious.
It is the fundamental emotion that stands at the cradle
of true art and true science."
—Albert Einstein

Albert Einstein, the German-Swiss physicist who became a United States citizen and was awarded the Nobel Prize for Physics in 1921, was one of the most remarkable scientists of the 20th century.

For all his incredible power of logic and unswerving allegiance to reason, Einstein was moved to claim that mystery was "the fundamental emotion."

Mystery implies that yet more learning and feeling lie beyond our present grasp. Mystery evokes both aspiration and humility before the unknown. Mystery brings us up short and drives us to our knees. Mystery can be embraced but never deciphered.

103
Sharpen, then Cut

"We cannot spend all our time sharpening the knife;
at some point we must cut."
—KARL RAHNER

Sharpening the knife is important. Otherwise, we will flail about with a dull instrument. Sometimes we're so riveted on slicing and butchering away that we bypass proper preparation.

Conversely, some folks are known to be perennial preparers. Given just a little more time or data or reflection, they will finally be ready to do some cutting. The knife could always be just a tad sharper. So these potential cutters spin around and around in endless circles of thought, with a usable, but unused, knife tightly clutched in their grasp.

The examined life, as they say, is rewarding, but the over-examined life isn't living.

Deal with the Details

"When I die, my epitaph should read: 'She paid her bills.'
That's the story of my private life."
—Gloria Swanson

Here's an actress, producer, businesswoman par excellence reflecting upon her home life. Life's always going to contain comical stretches and tragic turns, mysteries and science fiction, as well as absurd theatre and religious drama. There will be exceptional dimensions and twists to most of our journeys, but the heart of our lives has to do with how we play minor parts rather than await major roles.

Indeed, our lives are a mosaic of minor parts: dishwashing, transporting children, mending clothes, writing letters, taking walks, answering doorbells, visiting the sick, breaking bread with family, and performing a 100 such commonplace tasks.

I'm reminded of the legendary basketball coach John Wooden, who upon meeting his freshmen student-athletes would sit them down on benches in the locker room. "Then he told us," relates Hall of Fame talent Bill Walton, "exactly how he wanted us to don our socks, lace our shoes, and put on those shoes, to minimize blisters and the like." Coach Wooden would continue by showing the players how to tuck their jerseys in, tie the draw strings on their pants, dry their hair, warm up, eat properly, and even organize their day. This was all done before the players even got out on the court and took their first shots.

Deadlines. Details. Drudgery. Human existence is composed of all that. I challenge you to work not for hours but for objectives. For life mainly has to do with paying bills. On time.

105
Celebrate the Universal Birthday

Charles Lamb felt that New Year's Day symbolized every person's birthday. He was more accurate than he realized, for 98% of the atoms in our bodies weren't present one year ago. Hence, the start of a new year truly represents a golden opportunity to expand our ever-shifting identities. To do so, we could all benefit from a prayerful nudge. I offer this:

O Spirit of Infinite Love, a spirit both beyond our grasp yet filling our every corpuscle. Our souls are quivering before the enormous unknown of yet another year. Yes, we know that we can be responsible for our own mouth, our own heart, and our own actions. Yet we need buddies for the journey; consequently, we huddle together to garner strength from one another's thought and touch.

During the next year, may we offer others the bountiful bread of our beings. May our hearts be oiled with the healing balm of laughter. And may we remain hospitable to every foreign notion and fresh encounter.

Shalom, salaam, blessed be, namaste, and amen.

106
Go Dancing!

"We dance for pleasure and for the good of the city."
—ZUNI SAYING

There are societies so primitive as to have no apparel other than loin clothes, no tool other than stick or stone, no permanent dwellings, no carvings or plastic art, but nowhere on this planet can you find a people without music and dance. Indeed, the reality is that prehistoric religion was danced before it was stated. And as native cultures know: even a bad dance never hurts the earth.

So let our feet, hands, and overall body do some celebrating today. Notice the biblical King David who "danced before the Lord with all his might!" (II Samuel 6:14). Take a few minutes alone to express what is precious via movement. If dance makes you self-conscious then jog, bounce, ride a bicycle, or skateboard your spirit.

Life is composed of rhythmic movements: up and down, back and forth, yes and no, lifting and placing back down our hooves. To achieve physical and spiritual renewal, indeed for the dance to occur, both must occur daily.

For as Black Elk reminds: "Know that a vision has no power until it is danced before all the people."

107
Look for Surprises

"I am no scientist; I explore the neighborhood."
—Annie Dillard

A six-year-old girl said she had been getting up at the crack of dawn to "look for surprises," exploring her neighborhood. "But you can't expect surprises everyday," she was told; "they're reserved for special circumstances such as birthdays, Easter, Christmas, anniversaries, and Hanukkah."

"That's not true," she replied. "When I looked out the window yesterday I was surprised by a daffodil. And this morning I was surprised again, by a tulip down the block."

What most engaged our grandchildren, as youngsters, was Carolyn's lip balm or my guitar pick around which we would play interminably fascinating hide-and-seek games, including their dropping it in the belly of the guitar and my shaking the instrument wildly about until the pick popped out. We repeated this little game until one of us tired (guess who?), and after returning the pick to my coin purse, we'd scamper off to yet another surprise.

Grandchildren aren't preoccupied, like grownups, with hanging around for the so-called *big* joys of life; they're naturally focused on whatever lies right in front of them, "mounting to paradise by the stairway of surprise" (Emerson).

Small children shall lead us adults into worlds of splendor and astonishment. All of life is a wondrous spectacle, if we are but ready and receptive—in point of fact, engaging its surprises. Raymond Panikkar used to warn his students on the first day of his course in "Comparative Mysticism" that if they were not open to the possibility of utter surprise or being duly transformed during the semester, then they should immediately drop the course.

108
Don't Attempt to Dodge Death

"I'm not afraid to die. I just don't want to be there when it happens."
—WOODY ALLEN

Death, more so than money or sex, is our modern day taboo. We are a death-denying and death-defying culture. We loathe being reminded of our wrinkles or demise. It's difficult, sometimes unbearable, to discuss death, especially our own, in a frank and sensitive manner. One way to break the ice is to crack jokes about it. Woody Allen has made a livelihood out of laughing at and about death. His volumes and movies are packed with clever jabs at our mortality. Here's another one: "I don't believe in an afterlife, although I'm bringing a change of underwear."

Laughing about something serious can, of course, be exaggerated. We can get carried away and never face the reality. However, just the right amount of levity eases our anxieties and opens our minds to confronting our taboos.

There's another way of dealing with death. It's dealing with the little deaths—shrugs, departures, impasses—we face during the flow of a normal day of demands and crises. Every time we release or let go or say goodbye to something or someone we are practicing dying; we're warming up for the final farewell.

109

Pay Your Debts

"Owe no one anything, except to love one another; for they who have loved their neighbor have fulfilled the law."
—ROMANS 13:8

We incur many kinds of debts—economic, social, personal, and political ones. Moral debts too; for we're shareholders in the ethical expenses involved as members of the human commonwealth. Most of all, as the Romans declared, we owe one another our respect and affection. All other obligations are attached to this one. Truly, "love is the fulfilling of the law" (v. 10): the satisfaction of all other debts.

Here's my perspective: I can't, nor should I ever try, to write someone else's personal script, but I can contribute shards of savvy here and there, or sometimes even turn on the lights in the room, so that others might avoid stumbling. We aren't *responsible* for anyone else but ourselves, but we are *related* to everyone who shares the globe.

110
Spend Time in Your Backyard

"I've stayed in the front yard all my life. I want a peek at the
back where it's rough and untended and hungry
weeds grow. A girl gets sick of a rose."
—GWENDOLYN BROOKS

Fear keeps most of us stuck in the front yards of existence, where the lawn is tidy and neat, manicured. There we stay, rocking away in comfy chairs, waving to passersby, and rising only to admire or tend blooming gardens.

Brooks challenges herself, and us as well, to visit the backyards of our stories: where life grows unkempt, wild, and wooly. Full-fledged pilgrims smartly spend time in both yards, front and back, as well as visiting vacant lots and alleys too.

111
"The Body Never Lies."
—MARTHA GRAHAM

The cells, the shapes, and the twitches of our bodies are bona fide truth-tellers. Our well-being is rarely hidden but divulged in the open, for all to see, via our flesh and blood. I've also found that

---

whenever I wish to alter my being, my body is invariably involved, one way or another.

And remember we're all card-carrying members of TAB—the "temporarily able-bodied"—so dare to stretch your given body to its farthest reaches every day you walk the earth.

112

"Make Thyself Known…"

"The Delphic Oracle advised, 'Know thyself'; I would say, 'Make thyself known' and then thou wilt know thyself."
—SIDNEY JOURARD

We are more likely to know our beings through the process of revealing them. Total self-disclosure is neither possible nor desirable, but too many of us are walking, expurgated versions. We monitor and censor behavior and revelations in order to create an image of ourselves that we want others to have. We are obsessed with "looking good."

Alas, no one is helped in such phony, partial portrayals. Our neighbor may be temporarily fooled; but when we're counterfeit, both parties ultimately suffer.

Where do you currently find yourself on the continuum of knowing thyself *and* making thyself known?

113
Try Your Hand at Experimentation

"In a question of possibility, negative experience counts for nothing,
if there is but one, single, positive success!"
—WILLIAM ERNEST HOCKING

Thomas Edison saw one thing in his laboratory which indicated that a particular achievement was possible. So he experimented repeatedly without success, and a co-worker tried to console him with the statement, "It's too bad; all that work and no result." Edison replied with the now-famous remark, "What do you mean? We have lots of results; we know 700 things that won't work!"

Most productive scientists, inventors, and adventurers of the mind have always operated this way. Their psyches dwell in the greatest nation in the world: "the imagination" (James Durst). Always chasing the positive, they won't rest until they uncover a breakthrough, a single success. They refuse to enter the grave mouthing the two saddest words in any language: "If only, if only!"

114
Habit Is a Cable

"Sow an act and ye shall reap a habit; sow a habit and ye shall
reap a character, sow a character and ye shall reap a destiny."
—WILLIAM JAMES

It's not a question of having habits or not; we all have them, a bouquet of both lousy and satisfying ones. One of life's charges is to

---

maximize the positive ones while minimizing the negative habits. Then engage in what my psychotherapist friend, Charlie O'Leary, calls "the 5% rule":

> *Most of us have someone in our work or home life who wishes we would change five percent of our habits or change one of our habits five percent. If you don't believe this, ask someone if there is anything they would like to see more of or less of in your behavior.*

Too many of us want to stop something cold turkey or start something from scratch; it's tough to do, isn't it? Instead I follow the O'Leary 5% rule. What has worked for me is to build up to 5% by working on altering an attitude or behavior just a little bit, like 1%, for the first month, then another 1%, then another...

Or phrased similarly: habit is a cable. We weave a thread of it everyday, and, finally, it's woven so tightly, we're unable to break it.

115
There's a Season to Be Diplomatic

"Diplomacy is the skill in handling events without arousing hostility."
—Webster

Although we talk about diplomacy primarily in the political realm, its adroit handling is essential everywhere. We need to learn tact: how to touch one another with firm, friendly, and fair hands. Diplomacy, because it requires great dexterity, draws humorous portrayals. Here are but a few:

> *Diplomacy is the art of stepping on someone's shoes without spoiling the polish.*
> —Art Linkletter

Diplomacy is to do and say the nastiest thing in the nicest manner.
—ISAAC GOLDBERG

Diplomacy is the art of letting someone else have your way.
—ANONYMOUS

Being forthright is usually the best policy, but sometimes, like the coyote or trickster, we must unnerve or move obliquely to effect our desired result. Here's a telling illustration.

One evening in the long and illustrious life of Winston Churchill, he faced one of the most difficult diplomatic trials of his career. It seems that while attending an elegant dinner party, Churchill was approached by the distraught hostess who happened to observe one of the other guests pocketing one of her best silver salt and pepper shaker sets. She discreetly asked the great diplomat if he might think of some way to get them back without causing an unpleasant scene.

Shortly, Sir Winston went to the other end of the immense dining table, pocketed the other set of silver shakers, then sidled up to the thief. He opened his pocket just wide enough for the chap to see the shakers inside and whispered, "I think they've seen us, we'd better put them back."

116
You Are Your Deep, Driving Desires

"You are what your deep, driving desire is. As your deep,
driving desire is, so is your will. As your will is, so is your deed.
As your deed is, so is your destiny."
—THE UPANISHADS

After years of devoting his life to healing efforts, Carl Jung made an incisive observation about how people are and are not healed. He wrote: "All the greatest and most important problems of life are fundamentally insoluble. They can never be solved, but only outgrown. This outgrowing requires a new level of consciousness. Some higher or wider interest, a new and stronger life urge or desire, must appear on the patient's horizon."

People who join recovery movements often find that becoming clean or clear is crucial but inadequate for the worthwhile life. In fact, once they remove their addiction, their life can fall prey to emptiness. The way of healing, as Jung notes, is not only to halt, or even halve, certain desires, but, in fact, to replace them with new and healthier ones.

We are known by the deep, driving desires we keep.

117
"Do What You Can, with What You Have, Where You Are."
—THEODORE ROOSEVELT

Our powers are restricted. Our goals are tarnished. Nonetheless, inventive people make the most of their situations. They use what gifts lie *within* to accomplish what tasks lie *before* them.

The *can* has to do with outside limits, the *have* with inner capacity, and the *are* with present location. Limits, competence, and site are equally significant ingredients in one's commitment to action. Go with what you possess: remember that proficient woodworkers or pianists don't judge themselves because their hands have only 5 fingers, instead of 6 or 7; they manage with what they have.

Notice Roosevelt's first word: Do! He doesn't allow for weaseling, postponing, or emoting. Do! Roosevelt is urging us to quit

---

waiting until we're persuaded beyond a shadow of a doubt about any specific course of action, because that time never arrives. Life is finally not about yesterday or tomorrow but now. As my friend likes to say: "Salvation is not in the sweet by-and-by but in the nasty now-and-now."

When asked "what time is it, Yogi?" Berra replied: "You mean now?" Yes, Yogi, yes.

118

We All Could Use Directions

"The great thing in this world is not so much where we stand, as in what direction we are moving."
—OLIVER WENDELL HOLMES

It's related of a certain traveler, somewhere in northern Vermont, that after driving in uncertainty for a considerable spell, he became convinced he was on the wrong road, and so, at the first village, he came to a halt.

Calling one of the villagers to the car window, he said, "Friend, I need help. I'm lost." The villager looked at him for a moment. "Do you know where you are?" he asked. "Yes," said the traveler, "I saw the name of the village as I entered." The man nodded his head. "Do you know where you want to go?" "Yes," the traveler replied and named the destination. The villager looked away for a moment, ruminating. "You ain't lost," he said at last, "You just need directions."

Sometimes we need directions; other times we are the direction-giver. We will assume both roles during life's journey.

119
Founders Are Free yet Fettered Spirits

"Not one of the founders of the world religions was a dreamy,
undisciplined person lost in a beatnik atmosphere of
indolence and self-centeredness."
—ALFRED STIERNOTTE

Founders aren't merely idealists. If so, they would founder. There are dozens of seers who have wild imaginations and spin glorious possibility after possibility. But ambitions aren't harnessed without fortitude and luck. Founders are institutionalists. They generate their own dreams, or utilize the dreams of others, and do something creative with them. They lay foundations. They know that ideas must have legs. And they find common ground by moving the debate to a higher ground.

World religions that have endured have been the result of both inner searching and intense suffering. There aren't more than a dozen or so supreme religious leaders for the whole of humankind in the last 3000 years.

Perhaps it's the right time for you to risk founding something.

120
Get Down and Dirty

"You are so afraid of losing your moral sense that you are not willing to
take it through anything more dangerous than a mud puddle."
—GERTRUDE STEIN

The only way to stay clean is to stay clear of the messy ethical struggles confronting sensitive humans daily. Life dares people to soil, scuff, and sully their spiritual outfits.

Good athletes get down and dirty. They don't play dirty; they merely dirty their uniforms, due to fair yet aggressive moves. There's a time to stay in the dugouts, safe from the contest, but, sooner or later, the game of life must be played on the field, where there are acres of dirt.

Genuine servant-leaders also get grubby. I've been impressed by the fact that Emperor Hirohito could often be found, during the late afternoons, cleaning the restrooms of his headquarters. Ironically, no job was considered beneath this leader who purportedly stood above his populace. Hirohito was willing to dirty his hands bearing the marks of toil and struggle.

121
Take Advantage of Your Disappointments

*"As I look back over my life, I find no disappointment
and no sorrow I could afford to lose."*
—THEODORE PARKER

I wouldn't go that far. Shit happens, to be sure, but some of it fertilizes, while the rest of it just stinks up the place. There are certainly travesties in my life I could have done without, but I will concede that most of my disappointments and sorrows have been integral to my present spiritual condition.

I'm thankful for the time I messed in my pants in kindergarten. It was terribly embarrassing, but it wouldn't be the last time I felt that way. Plus it served early notice that I wouldn't always be in control of my life.

I'm thankful for that agonizing 4-3 defeat in Little League, the only scar on our otherwise unblemished record back in 1952. Later on, in college, when our undistinguished basketball team lost 21 straight contests, I finally internalized the wisdom that no form of "perfection" was in the cards for me. My favored and relatively unscathed upbringing needed such jolts of reality.

I'm thankful for my painful divorce that drove home many lessons: my capacity for ugliness, my need to give and receive forgiveness, and my ability to rise, as a phoenix, from the ashes.

I'm thankful for the loss of my job in 1973, the rejection of my essay in 1981, the award never received in 1985, and the criticisms you and you and you continue to send my way, or as my friend says: "You just delivered a lesson to me by being such a pain, so thanks."

There are plenty more personal disappointments and sorrows to mention, but it's your turn now.

122
"We Are Born Originals, yet We Die Copies."
—EDWARD YOUNG

We die copies, because we've been hoodwinked into believing that we aren't good enough as we are. We're socialized to imitate this or that part of model persons. We can follow others and learn from them, but it remains bad advice to copy others. Our sole job, for one entire lifetime, is to fulfill our peculiar destiny.

The uniqueness of each situation and person is tirelessly stressed in Hasidism. Accused by the congregation of altering the service that he inherited from his father, one Hasidic master rejoined, "I do exactly as my father did. He did not imitate, and neither do I!"

Phony, insecure religious autocrats in history have always sought not followers but copiers. Genuine holy people are not trapped in ego-extension. They express religiosity in their own singular ways, and, more importantly, invite us to follow suit.

Buddha's final words, upon his death bed, invoked us to "put no head above your own, not even mine. Be a lamp unto yourself" (literally, "make of yourself a light"). It was the disciples who came after Buddha who gravitated to conformity and imitation.

123
Improve, then Improve Some More

"There's always room for improvement.
It's the biggest room in the house."
—Louise Heath Leber

Particular rooms within my favorite homes have brought me delight and solace. I sought aloneness, and a corner furnished it. I wished to express my creative impulses, and I made a room over in my own image.

I invite you to wander leisurely about your current residence and discover anew those spots that console or disturb you. As appropriate, be willing to rearrange your quarters to meet present aspirations. Alter your environs.

There are physical and emotional rooms inside our homes and hearts. The challenge, while alive, is to provide both with treasures that are beautiful and that match our spirit.

As the Zen Master noted: "All of you students are perfect just as you are and you could all use a little improvement."

124
Be Discerning

I heard of the barber who refused to give a discount to a bald client, declaring that his artistry consisted not in the cutting but in the knowing when to stop. That's so true of countless endeavors: perceiving when to launch, when to continue, and when to cease… be it bonds or tasks.

Theodore Geisel, known as Dr. Seuss, the beloved author of children's books, was chosen by the Lake Forest College graduating class years back to be their commencement speaker. Geisel approached the podium and announced that he'd been researching the function of a commencement address ever since being notified of his selection. A speaker, he'd found, should give the graduates all he or she knew of the world's wisdom.

So here's the speech in its entirety that was delivered by Dr. Seuss on that august occasion:

My uncle ordered popovers from the restaurant's bill of fare.
And when they were served, he surveyed them with a penetrating stare.
Then he spoke great words of wisdom as he sat there on that chair:
"To eat those things you must exercise great care.
You may swallow down what's solid, but you must spit out the air."

And as you partake of the world's bill of fare,
That's darn good advice to follow.
Do a lot of spitting out of the hot air.
And be careful what you swallow.

As we partake of the world's incredible bill of fare, we must be discerning. We must select this and reject that. We need to stand up for this value and repudiate that one. We are called to spit out the hot air while being careful what we swallow.

"Speak to the Children of Israel that They Go Forward."
—Exodus 14:15

FIDO, which stands for "forget it, drive on," is a sports slogan that carries coinage in all spheres of life. We must forge ahead, no matter what happens in the moment—be it a blessing or a curse. Keep on keeping on...

John Haynes Holmes once commented on three kinds of people among the Israelites during their march through the desert.

One group wanted to go back to Egypt. They preferred slavery to the uncertainty of the wilderness. The second group was satisfied with wherever they might camp at night. They were content to gather the manna as it came. The third group, the smallest, wanted to go forward. Moses was among their number. He heard God say to him, "Speak to the children of Israel that they go forward." And Moses internalized that mandate.

In our own tongue, these are respectively the spiritual and social reactionaries, conservatives, and progressives. They are the people of yesterday, today, and tomorrow. Frankly, I find myself situated in all three states. Upon more than one occasion, I've felt them battling one another for ascendancy in my being.

Life sometimes entails being caught in a storm of live coals, hot ashes, and boiling mud. And I struggle to go forward. How about you?

126

"Disorder Is Here to Stay."

In Saul Bellows' book *Humboldt's Gift*, Charlie Citrine reminds an overly optimistic friend that "disorder is here to stay." We clamor for perfect calm and stability. We seek to manage unreasonable persons or harness uncontainable events. Worse yet, we believe we can do so. We keep on wanting to "still-photo" our lives when things are going swell. We want to capture existence like that forever, preserving it against every whim or misfortune. But life doesn't work that way.

Our emotional states are never purely mad, sad, or glad; they're wacky mixtures. Disorder is here to stay, and the best we can do is cultivate our local patches of turf, holding the principalities and powers at bay for awhile.

Nothing is safe forever, but much is enjoyable along the way.

127

Crayons Are Our Teachers

"We could learn a lot from crayons: some are sharp, some are pretty, some are dull, some have odd names, and all are different colors, but they all have to learn to live in the same box."
—ANDY ROONEY

The world is truly becoming increasingly diverse in every way: economically, racially, religiously, and in terms of every conceivable life-style. Diverse literally means "turned in different ways"; so our human reality has diversified indeed. There exists a pluralism of skin colors, sexual orientations, simply countless ways of being our authentic selves. The mission of the ripened person is not merely to tolerate such diversity but to celebrate it as the result of an evolving universe.

But there remain holdouts. "Who was the first man, Bobby?" asked the teacher. "George Washington," answered Bobby promptly. "Why, no, Bobby," exclaimed the teacher. "You ought to know better. Adam was the first man."

"Oh, well," said Bobby, determined to prove himself right. "I wasn't counting foreigners!" Well, foreigners do count, Bobby. Everyone counts, and all of our children must be taught that primary lesson.

George Washington and Martha Washington, Adam and Eve, Palestinians and Israelis, Americans and North Koreans, Susan and Bobby are all members of the same human family and to be treated as such. Let's not split hairs over which race was first in history. After all, the only race that really matters is the full human race.

128

"Hold Fast to Dreams..."

"Hold fast to dreams, for if dreams die, life is a broken-winged bird that cannot fly."
—LANGSTON HUGHES

Name your aspirations and dreams. Some are unrealizable; accept them as such and let them pass quietly. Others are achievable but not significant enough to hold fast. You may revisit them later, but for now, discard them. Which dreams remain? Which ones are for the world, for your loved ones, or pertain solely to you?

Here's a prime example of tapping into one's truest and broadest dream. During the 1963 March on Washington, Martin Luther King, Jr. hadn't locked into the usual power that his speeches ordinarily conveyed. Singer Mahalia Jackson, seated just behind King on the podium, leaned in as King seemed to be sputtering, and passionately exhorted him, "Tell them about the dream, Martin, tell them about the dream!" Her urging led to King reframing his entire message. King then proceeded to muster one of the finest, most important, talks ever delivered in American history. His "I Have a Dream" speech energized the racial justice revolution in our land.

Few possess either King's genius or mission, but we all harbor powerful, realizable dreams for self and others. Do something modest toward actualizing one dream today, for huge accomplishments often begin in humble ways.

129
Gentleness and Strength Are Yoked

"It is the weak who are cruel. Gentleness can
only be expected from the strong."
—Leo Rosten

When we're weak, we lash out. Our insecurity impels us to bring others to their knees. Parents overpower children out of weakness. So do bullies operating at school, at work, or on the international scene.

When we're strong, we have no need to demean or injure another. When we're strong, we don't have to flex muscles. When we're strong, we don't hanker to be cruel, even toward foes. When we're strong, we can be temperate and tender.

One of my colleagues, Harry Meserve, once quoted a psychologist on the art of sermonizing, who suggested from the pew: "Rub folks gently where it hurts." Particularly when the preacher has something difficult to convey, it must be shared in a soft and easy fashion for the message to arrive successfully. Or as one of my mentors warned me: "Tom, as a preacher, you will unavoidably step on some toes every Sunday. Just try not to step on the same ones two weeks in a row!"

130
Drop It!

The Buddha was sought out by an ardent follower bringing presents to show devotion to the Master. Gotama gave her an audience. The woman stepped forward and held out her right hand, offering a priceless ivory ornament. "Drop it," said Buddha.

The surprised woman obeyed and stepped back. Then she stepped forward again, this time offering in her left hand a precious jewel. "Drop it," said Buddha. Again the disciple, flabbergasted, obeyed and stepped back.

Then, smiling as if catching the Buddha's meaning, she held out both hands empty and stepped forward. "Drop it," said Buddha.

What do we prize most: our talents, possessions, independence, prestige, our…? Sometimes all we have must be laid aside, consciously and voluntarily. Our hands must be empty if we are to receive and empty if we are to give.

131
"Speak to the Earth and It Shall Teach Thee."
—Job 12:8

Slowly yet relentlessly, over the centuries, we have abused our environment. We have used the resources of our ecosystem without thoughtfulness or care. We have not been gracious unto our kin, the earth. We are only now realizing the organic view; namely, that we are part of an entire web, and if a segment is broken or torn, the whole web shudders.

We humans must repent and reconnect. Being green means being both reverential *and* subversive, simultaneously. We must acknowledge, in the marrow of our bones, that we are a product of nature. We are of the soil, we are of the sea, and we are of the air. We are interdependent.

Let us speak to the earth with the voices of body and soul, and then, after having our say, listen attentively to it, for it shall teach us. Remember the words of the Sioux holy one, Black Elk: "The earth is sacred and is a relative of ours."

132
Take and Pass the Easter Exam

If you want to get to the nubbins of a person's theology, you must heed their Easter message. One of my ministerial friends, Greg Ward, is a man whom I've been blessed to know ever since he was eight years old, when I served as his minister some 40+ years ago. Rev. Greg has a litmus test he calls the "Easter Exam," which we're invited to pass every year. It shows that love is possible in a hard and hurting world. And we need to take the Easter Exam not just annually but over and over again.

Indeed, whatever one believes or doesn't believe about any bodily resurrection, our lives are deepened only when we can honestly announce, then embody, that love is stronger even than death, that love outlives death, and here's not only the life of a Jewish rabbi to confirm it...but more importantly here's the proof of my own odyssey.

133
Intimacy Crackles!

"With the exception of only a very few situations, there adheres
to the tenderest and most intimate of our love-relations
a small portion of hostility."
—SIGMUND FREUD

This truth is hard to swallow. But the fact remains that intimacy crackles, rubs us raw, and occasionally incites scratching, even clashing. A marriage authority claims that even with happy couples, 70% of their major issues never get solved, let alone resolved; they are merely dealt with continuously. In healthy sparring, the bickering, while incessant, is out in the open and regularly faced.

Frankly, I'm satisfied that I married in Carolyn, my second wife, a person with an expansive not flat temperament; hence, we've enjoyed countless sparks of both delight and frustration during our 39 years of marriage.

After a heated argument with her husband, a woman said, "Why can't we live peacefully like our two dogs do most of the time?" "Yes, they don't fight that much, but tie them together and let's see what happens."

Hale and hearty partnerships scrap yet keep on improving.

134
We Are What We Eat

*"So beautiful a sound, the crust breaks up like manna and falls all over
everything, and then we eat. Bread gets inside humans. "*
—DANIEL BERRIGAN

We are in the midst of a nutritional revolution. A new food consciousness is upon us. There is a conspiracy against fatness. We're
becoming more ethical and enlightened eaters. We're willing to
confess that we *are* what we eat. At every meal we aspire to enhance
our nutrient absorption.

Eating is at the heart of religion as well as personal identity.
In the Hebrew scriptures, at every turn, God is either sitting down
to table or setting one up for others. And the Last Supper is a celebration full of affection, food, betrayal, remembrance, hope, and
anxiety.

An excellent example of the ubiquitous eating-together motif
in the Bible is where the realm of God is described as a huge banquet hall and people are invited to show up from the North and
South and East and West (not just one parochial region), sit down,
and feast one with another. And there will be plenty of folks present who weren't mentioned on your or my guest list. Imagine that!

The Gaelic word for family means "those who eat together."
And the English word *companion* is derived from a Latin phrase
"those who share bread." When we cut ourselves off from mutual,
sacred meals, we cut ourselves off from vital nourishment.

135
Make the Extra Effort

"On some days a player only feels 70% okay,
but I still want 100% of their 70%."
—BASEBALL COACH

When our grandson Trevor was about 5 years old, he started going to professional baseball games with us. He still does, now that he nears 17. He also plays on his high school baseball team. Baseball permeates his blood and body.

After one of his first appearances at Qualcomm Stadium, following a Padres major league game, we went to the car, got inside, and, despite being tuckered out, Trevor's first words were: "Two things are important, Grandpa: keep your eye on the ball, and if you're a little scared, it's alright!" Yes and yes. Then Trevor fell soundly asleep on the trip back home.

Later on, in Little League, he and I came up with an acronym: F.A.C.E., which stands for Focus, Accuracy, Consistency, and Effort. Well, to be truthful, I came up with it. Then just last year on Trevor's frosh baseball team, the coach said: "Okay, players, the word *success* comes before *work* only one time in life. Where is that true?" The players grew silent. The coach bellowed: "Only in the dictionary, only in the dictionary!"

Together, young and old, with immense sweat and despite being understandably frightened, we can grow a wondrous world, can't we?

136
It Isn't Always Greener Elsewhere

"Hey, I hear there's a hell of a universe next door. Let's go."
—E. E. CUMMINGS

The anecdote runs that the mother of three notoriously unruly youngsters was asked whether or not she'd have children if she had it to do over again. "Oh, yes," she replied, "but maybe not the same ones."

The reality is that certain parents and certain children don't mesh, never have and never will. It's as if they've arrived from different planets. Having confessed that, there is too much tendency in our modern world to pursue serial jobs and rotating relationships in hopes of finding the perfect place or person. Such a pursuit will end in disappointment. We would do well to heed the counsel of the poet Wendell Berry: "Be like a tree: stand firm, grip hard, thrust upward, bend to the winds of heaven and learn tranquility." In short, grow where you're planted!

Life is hardly ever greener on the other side of the fence. We merely encounter different problems elsewhere as well as carry our own snags and troubles with us.

137
Start with a Taste of Honey

In Judaism when a youngster first studies the Torah, after the initial word, they are given a taste of honey so they will associate learning with sweetness. What a grand way to launch the education of any child! Children need to know that life can be sweet, that they are inherently worthwhile and good, and that learning can be a delightful adventure, right from the git-go. Soon enough our little ones will be exposed to life's bitterness and gristle or, conversely, to an avalanche of cotton candy.

A taste of honey provides just the right start.

138
Be an Embeddual

"People need not be glued together when they belong together."
—SIGMUND FREUD

Psychologist Robert Kegan, in his book *The Evolving Self,* depicts human beings, in an evocative phrase, as "embedduals." This coined term means we're independent and separate as well as connected and social creatures. We're individuals deeply embedded in the various structures of the universe.

We need to nourish both our singleness and our commonality on the road toward full personhood. Self-enrichment alone is insufficient.

Ralph Waldo Emerson, who was known for his dogged self-reliance, according to biographers, was also a good neighbor, devoted citizen, affectionate father, loyal brother, and a man surrounded with friends. He was an embeddual, to be sure. In fact, as a child Ralph Waldo once watched a sawyer cutting up some wood. The task was beyond young Emerson's strength, but finally he saw a way to be useful. "May I," Emerson asked, "do the grunting for you?"

139
Make Peace with Reality

Here's an illustrative story about the woman in Budapest who goes to her rabbi with a complaint: "Life is unbearable. There are nine of us living in one room. What can I do?" The rabbi answers, "Take your goat into the room with you." The woman is incredulous, but the rabbi insists: "Do as I say and come back in a week."

A week later the woman comes back, looking more agitated than before. "We cannot stand it," she tells the rabbi. "The goat is filthy." The rabbi then tells her, "Go home and let the goat out. And come back in a week."

A radiant woman returns to the rabbi a week later, exclaiming: "Life is beautiful. We enjoy every minute of it now that there's no goat, only the nine of us!" Yes, equanimity would exhort us to accept life as it is, to make sufficient peace with our existing conditions. Sometimes we have to quit fighting reality.

140
May Our Words Become Flesh

"My life, my argument."
—ALBERT SCHWEITZER

Albert Schweitzer, the epitome of an embodied life, humbly noted: "I am only a person living out my religion." You see, he believed in turning his creeds into deeds. As the Gospel of John states: "The Word became flesh." God's love for the world became flesh (literally "tabernacled" or "pitched tent" in our midst), was born in

Jesus the Nazarene. This is a faith-claim that the same Spirit that covenanted with Moses, argued with Gideon, struggled within Jeremiah…that same Spirit had returned, incarnating a fresh and robust love in the Bethlehem birth.

Our words are wasted until they become flesh: that's the core message of the Christian faith, I dare say, of all world religions. Oh, the many words—good and righteous words—we mouth in abundance during the course of our lives, words that unfortunately seldom become flesh, remaining but pious platitudes. John reminds us to enflesh some of our noble sentiments. When we merely have ideas, they're often subdued and wooden, but when ideas grasp us, then they can become flesh and catch fire.

Saying the word "love" is mere warm-up for "loving."

141
Grow Enlightened

"After enlightenment, the laundry."
—JACK KORNFIELD

A young monk approached his Roshi and asked him what it was that he did before he gained enlightenment. The Roshi answered, "Before I was enlightened, I chopped wood and fetched water. Now that I am enlightened, I chop wood and fetch water."

Too many people seeking enlightenment feel that once they reach "it," their life activities will alter radically. On the contrary, when we obtain any measure of wisdom, we merely grant greater density to the tasks in which we're already engaged.

Enlightened people don't do different things so much as they do the same things differently—perchance with more verve, lightheartedness, and perspective.

142
Open Up

"Behold, I set before you an open door which no one is able to shut."
—Rev. 3:8

One of the first sermons I ever delivered, back in 1965, was based on the biblical passage where the Aramaic word *ephphatha* (meaning "be opened") was uttered by Jesus upon healing the man who was deaf and dumb (Mark 7:34). This exhortation has posed a core invitation throughout my journey.

In fact, at the beginning of every worship service, I extend a ritual that says: "we are a people of open minds, loving hearts, and helping hands." For once we open up our hearts, heads, and hands, it's increasingly difficult to shut or close ourselves back up.

The rabbis of old put it this way: we come into existence with our fists clenched, but when we die, our hands are wide open. The purpose of life is to keep gradually opening up our entire beings, all along the road.

143
"What I Gave, I Have."

*"What I kept, I lost. What I spent, I had.
What I gave, I have."*
—English Gravestone

The art of keeping can be a useful habit. There will always be secrets to keep, treasures to store, and memories to harbor. But some of us stash compulsively; we keep, keep, keep. We develop into full-blown hoarders. We stockpile objects, while losing the joy of possession.

To spend means to use up or pay out: in either case, we expend, maybe even exhaust, resources, if not ourselves. However, at least in spending we no longer withhold or conceal something.

This English epitaph closes by reminding us that, when we depart life, we only have what we gave and shared in love and trust. I think of my burgeoning sheet music collection. I can't take it with me (that is, keep it forever). I don't want to sell or trade it in. I merely want to give it to my children or someone who would cherish it. Then we will both harbor something in common: a bond of love and memory.

And then there are my two guitars and my photo albums and my baseball memorabilia and our house and...

144
"Only the Hand that Erases Can Write the True Thing."
—Meister Eckhart

Ralph Waldo Emerson was a Unitarian preacher for a short spell, before he left the ministry for writing and lecturing. Among other things, the priestly and pastoral portfolios didn't appeal to Emerson, so he abandoned his initial vocation for a better fit.

Near the end of his active literary career, Emerson did some circuit riding. He would preach at various congregations, employing some of his old sermons. Waldo would come to a certain part of the sermon and pensively remark: "Well, I don't believe that anymore," then he would go on to offer a current amendment to his former text.

In our quest for truth we must be willing to revise earlier insights. This is more readily recommended than actually accomplished. It can take immense bravery to say farewell to our intellectual offspring of yore.

145

Be Erotic Rather than Sexy

Nearly five decades ago, during my training as a campus ministry intern, I delivered a sermon that was enthusiastically received. The Dean of the Chapel even urged me to send it off to *Pulpit* magazine for possible publication. However, first he wanted me to run it by his friend, Ed Warner, former editor of *Pulpit*. Warner scrutinized it, then called me over to his home for comments. His words were blunt, almost blistering, to the ears of this green-horn seminarian: "Tom, your sermon is sexy but rarely erotic!"

Warner proceeded to demonstrate convincingly where it was sexy: where the language was showy, even titillated the mind; where the style was shiny enough to sell and be bought; where the content swiveled and was succulent but failed to exude vitality; and where the sermon crackled but couldn't sustain its blaze. His critique proved scathingly accurate not just about this lone sermon but about my overall life at the time.

Moreover, Warner evinced a truth relevant to our greater society. The trouble with most contemporary women and men is not that we feel too much passion, but that we don't access our passion sufficiently. We grow disconnected from our erotic wellsprings. Sexiness by itself prompts us to be scintillating and juicy without risking concomitant tenderness. The lover, when fueled by *eros*, desires to touch and be touched with primal knowing, beneath the surface, with inner ardor.

146
"Lieben und Arbeiten"

Sigmund Freud was asked what he thought a normal person should be able to do well in life. His answer came quickly: "*lieben und arbeiten*," namely, to love and to work. These two primary human tasks are often inseparable. I find that I love myself and others most while being productive, and, similarly, I am happiest at work when my affectional needs are being met.

In our vocations we search for daily meaning as well as daily bread. We desire recognition every bit as much as remuneration. We yearn to inquire as well as acquire.

Life is pretty basic: may we love our work and labor at our loving.

147
Fail Forward

"'Another ball game lost! Good grief! I get tired of losing...everything I do, I lose!' 'Look at it this way, Charlie Brown,' says Lucy, 'we can learn more from losing than we do from winning!' 'Hey, then that makes me the smartest person in the world!'"
—CHARLES SCHULZ

Poor Charlie Brown could use a few more successes under his belt in order to transform his defeatist attitude. Conversely, most of us need permission to lose, the right to be wrong, the green light not to be perfect. We need freedom to fail even when it really hurts, where much is at stake, in "performance" areas such as academics, sexuality, work, and parenting. We need to lose without giving ourselves the label "loser."

If we respect ourselves, then mistakes aren't likely to damage our identity. We will maximize the lessons learned from our blunders. Our losses become instructive rather than injurious.

It's called the art of failing forward.

148
Renounce Kvetching

"Therefore encourage one another and build one another up."
—I THESSALONIANS 5:1

Kvetching is a Yiddish term for habitually complaining, griping, and grousing about most everyone and everything. It's a condition that breeds ulcers and spoils bonds. Instead of kvetching, we need to convert the majority of our yelps into helps. As my friend says, there are 10 rules for getting rid of the blues: go out and do something for someone else, then repeat it nine times with the same person or with several other fellow travelers.

We're placed on earth not to be kvetchers but to be *encouragers*, literally those willing to instill courage in the bodies and souls of our neighbors.

"Let Your Laughter Ring Forth."

"Keep fightin' for freedom and justice,
beloveds, but don't forget
to have fun doin' it.
Lord, let your laughter ring forth."
—MOLLY IVINS

My professor friend relates that among the Kurnai of Australia dwells a myth in which the waters of the earth had been swallowed by a great frog named Dak. The thirsty animals tried to get Dak to cough up the waters, but their efforts were in vain. Dak remained stubborn.

Finally the snake began twisting rolling about in a most comical fashion. Dak tried to maintain a straight face with resolve but couldn't, where upon he burst out laughing, and the waters streamed forth to soak the parched earth.

Laughter is sometimes that way. It bursts through worlds of sedateness and self-importance and allows the waters of life to flow freely to all, relieving the dryness and barrenness of our parched spirits.

Undoubtedly, truth without laughter has been a prime source of religious persecutions, political imprisonments, and even acts of genocide. Whether one is a Democrat or Republican, atheist or theist, Marxist or capitalist, Protestant or Catholic, revolutionary or reactionary, a sense of perspective and flexibility must be maintained. The best way to accomplish this ethical feat is through humor.

The humorist, Charles Lindner, puts it aptly: "A person has two legs and one sense of humor, and if you're faced with the choice, it's better to lose a leg." But a sobering truth remains: children

---

laugh about 400 times a day, while we adults average a mere 25 chuckles. Clearly, we've got a long way to go to lighten up, properly jiggle our innards, and let our laughter ring forth.

150

Life's Not Fair!

A little five-year-old girl came crying to her mother: "Billy took the biggest piece of cake, and it's not fair, because he was eating cake three years before I was even born."

My brother and I used to scrap over who got the biggest piece of cake or pie too. I never thought to use the argument of the aforementioned five-year-old, but it would have fit perfectly, because Phil is approximately three years older than I. We finally worked out a compromise whereby one of us would cut the cake and the other would make the selection. To make it even fairer Phil and I would trade off the duties each time we relished a dessert.

I hate to admit it, but one of my many foibles is that I still continue to eyeball (surreptitiously, if possible) dessert slices at mealtimes just to make sure I'm not being cheated. Parsimonious is the fancy word; stingy is the familiar one. Not one of my finer qualities, to be sure.

In my stronger moments, however, I abide by two slabs of wisdom: (1) Who said life was fair? and (2) We're called to live well with what we have rather than covet what we don't have!

Maybe I'm growing up a bit!

151
Faith Is More Verb than Noun

"Belief clings, but faith lets go."
—ALAN WATTS

An Hasidic rabbi once said: "To attain truth, one must pass forty nine gates, each opening onto a new questions, only to arrive finally before the last gate, the last question, beyond which one could not live without faith." A mature religion is one that takes reasonable steps of faith rather than negotiating wild leaps of credulity. Religion grows out of our best hunches and then goads us to take action. For our faith is only fulfilled in commitment.

Another Jewish legend reports that when Moses threw the wand into the Red Sea, the sea didn't divide itself to leave a dry passage for the Jews to cross. Not until the first person had stepped into the sea did the promised miracle happen and the waves recede.

Faith is more of a verb than a noun. You *faith* something into reality: you get up, rather than stay stuck; you keep going, even if shaky or wobbling some; you move ahead, even when unsure. You faith…step by step by step right out into the swirling sea.

152
Soak in Underrated Pleasures

In her book *My Mother's Body* the poet Marge Piercy notes "Six Underrated Pleasures: planting bulbs, sleeping with cats, canning, taking a hot bath, folding sheets and picking pole beans." And Anne Sexton in her poem "Welcome Morning" sings the praises of God

---

being present in the eggs, the kettle, the spoon, the chair, and the table of her morning rituals.

Here's what might make my top-six list (although I'm wide open to whimsical amendments down the homestretch): daydreaming, singing romantic ballads, chomping popcorn at a movie, sauntering around the block with our grandchildren, watching a live professional tennis match, taking a nap, mastering a mulish magic trick…Whoops, I came up with seven!

What would reside on your list of underrated pleasures?

153
Fame Can Be Fickle

TV news anchor Tom Brokaw was wandering through Bloomingdales in New York City one day, shortly after he was promoted to co-host on the *Today* show. That assignment was a pinnacle of sorts for Brokaw at the time, after years of work, first in Omaha, then for NBC in Los Angeles and Washington, and he was feeling mighty good about himself. Brokaw noticed a man watching him closely. The guy kept staring at Brokaw and finally, when the man approached him, Brokaw was sure he was about to reap the first fruits of being a New York television celebrity.

The man pointed his finger and said, "Tom Brokaw, right? "Right," said Brokaw. "You used to do the morning news on KMTV in Omaha, right?" "That's right," said Brokaw, getting set for the accolades to follow. "I knew it, I knew it the minute I spotted you," the fellow said. Then he paused and added, "Hey, whatever happened to you?"

Oh, fame can be flighty and fickle, can't it? There's always someone around to puncture our grand balloon. It's downright humbling to note that the present moment happens only once, and the Psalmist is spot on when he announces:

"We last no longer than a dream. We're like dry weeds that sprout in the morning, that grow and burst into bloom, then dry up and die in the evening."

—PSALM 90:5-6

154
Scout around for the Rocks

Noting the string of miraculous victories by the basketball team coached by Bob Dye, they asked him if he could somehow walk on water. He replied: "Hardly. But I do know where the rocks are!" Bob Dye doesn't coach anymore, but he was certainly a fine mentor. Dye knew which players to prod and which ones to pacify in order to maximize his team's overall success.

His retort about miracles is relevant to all of life. Seldom, if ever, will we mortals be able to perform biblical feats. Nonetheless, there are isolated instances in human history, today included, when individuals perform moral miracles equivalent to walking on water or raising the dead. We cradle untapped powers beyond our imagining.

While some wait around for earth-sized miracles to occur, others of us go forth looking for the rocks. Rest assured, there are lots to be found.

155
Familiarity Often Breeds Fondness

Gilbert Chesterton was seen chasing his hat in the street. Plunging through the traffic, a passer-by rescued it at his own peril and wasn't pleased when Gilbert remarked that his wife had just bought him a new one and would be sorry to see it again. "Then why on earth did you run after it?" "Well, it's an old friend. I am fond of it, and I wanted to be with it at the end."

We are a throw-away culture majoring in planned obsolescence. We're *novophiles,* zealously looking for the latest fad and newest object. Yet, in all of our lives, there exist treasures from yesteryear, objects that have become old friends, things that we choose to clutch and cherish until the end.

What are those old friends in your life, both animate and inanimate objects, that nourish rather than deaden your spirit?

The old line "familiarity breeds contempt" is rarely accurate in my life. In fine arts my fondness for certain paintings or musical pieces grows with increased exposure. Even some of the raucous contemporary music enjoyed by the younger generation has grown on me.

156
Worry Is Like a Rocking Chair

"I am old and have known a great many troubles,
but most of them never happened."
—MARK TWAIN

Thomas Kepler tells about the woman who realized that fears were ruining her life, so she made for herself a "worry table." In tabulating her worries, she discovered these eye-popping figures:

- 40% will never happen; anxiety is the result of mental fatigue
- 30% were about old decisions that we can't alter
- 12% constituted other people's criticism of us, often untrue or based on jealousy
- 10% were worries about our health, which gets worse the more we worry about it
- 8% were "legitimate," both private and public worries, since life poses real trials and tribulations

As they say, worry is like a rocking chair; it may give you something to sit in while mulling things over, but it won't take you anywhere.

157

"See the World Feelingly..."

"Rule #1 is this: nobody ever knows just how much another person hurts."
—Philip Booth

The tears of another may even run down our face or their smile curl on our own mouth. We can vicariously experience what another human being is going through. We can even occasionally understand it, even empathize with their plight, but we can never fully identify with it. We should never presume to know, let alone judge, the journey of our neighbor.

Although we're distinct creatures, you and I, it's customarily

---

wise, as well as compassionate, to "see the world feelingly" as does the blind person in the Shakespearean play *King Lear*.

158
Truth Is an Increasing Complexity

"There is no 'the truth.' Truth is not one thing or even a system.
It is an increasing complexity."
—ADRIENNE RICH

The commandment urging us not to bear false witness against our neighbor, although referring explicitly to the judicial system, would plead for integrity in every arena of life. Absolute honesty may not always be the best policy, yet we need to cry foul whenever we hear a press official claim that "our government has an inalienable right to lie."

A phrase from the Christian scriptures strikes a golden mean between brutal truthfulness and destructive duplicity when it exhorts us "to speak the truth in love." In sum, honesty must dwell in service of compassion. But in practice, the lines are fuzzy. We inhabit the gray zones and always will.

And remember, as Jewish theologian, Martin Buber, reports: we never garner any final or ultimate truth; we experience only "moment truths." And they shall suffice.

159
Live in Your Fingertips

I happened upon the notion that what we do with our fingertips (the ends of our wings) is where our soul emerges. It makes sense. For example, in gardening, playing the guitar, making crafts, performing magic, or baking bread, I'm dwelling in the zone of my fingertips...of soulfulness.

I also think of our beloved son, Russ, who has recently arrived at the rank of flight captain after numerous years of preparation and piloting–consummating his life-long dream. Every time Russ enters the cockpit, he's ultimately accountable for the well-being of a $70 million machine saddled with $2 billion worth of liability. Whether taking-off, cruising, or landing, Russ's proficiency as an airplane pilot banks squarely on the skillfulness of both his mind and his fingertips.

How do you spend time in your fingertips?

160
Run As Fast As You Can!

Years back, we went to our son's first competitive athletic event, a cross-country meet attracting 40+ schools from Santa Ana to Brawley. Russ's San Diego High team was strutting about in their beautiful blue sweatsuits, and Carolyn and I were already in tears. We would typically weep at our older children's track meets as well, even when son Chris got confused once and ran the wrong way during a relay.

Anyway, Russ's team finished somewhere in the middle of the

pack, and so did he. It turned out to be a teaching moment, made even grander by his mature perception, following the event, that there would always be runners faster and slower than he. Nonetheless, Russ vowed to do his darnedest to better his personal time and help his team in the races ahead.

Our older daughter, Jenny, who, after competing in an all-comers track meet, was asked by an adult friend, "How fast did you run?" replied: "As fast as I could!"

As fast as we can. As fine as we choose.

161
Merrymaking Is an Occupation

And Elijah said to Berokah, "These two will also share in the world to come." Berokah then asked them, "What is your occupation?" They replied, "We are merrymakers. When we see people downhearted, we cheer them up!"
—TALMUD

There is no greater calling than becoming a merrymaker, a bringer of joy into the depressed nooks and crannies of existence. Did you know that comedians are generally sad people off stage? Conversely, some plaintive leaders in society are comical in their private lives.

As it says in Proverbs 17:32: "A merry heart doeth good like a medicine, but a broken spirit drieth the bones." Now that I'm formally retired, I plan to keep my bones lubricated and loose. I'll put "merrymaker" by my name on any calling card. My merrymaking will include performing magic, feeding the homeless, singing in nursing homes, tutoring children, playing tennis and the guitar, just being "on call" to create glee and jollity wherever and whenever needed.

162
Remain Flexible

*"I can't put my finger on exactly what my philosophy
is now, but I'm flexible."*
—MALCOLM X

These words arrive from one of the initially rigid revolutionaries of our epoch. It shows that even the dogmatic among us can mellow and exhibit moments of elasticity in thought and deed.

Flexibility is the true sign, not of weakness, but of strength. I wish statespersons and people in places of power were willing to display such malleability as Malcolm X did in his maturing years. He wasn't a flimflammer, but he displayed true resilience, the capacity to either spring back to one's original shape or bounce ahead to new possibilities.

Tragically, just as Malcolm X was exhibiting signs of conciliatory change, he was assassinated.

163
Develop a Good Forgettery

Clara Barton (1821-1912) the founder and president of the U.S. Red Cross was never one to bear grudges. Being reminded by a friend of a wrong done to her some years earlier: "Don't you remember?" asked her friend. "No," Clara replied firmly, "I distinctly remember forgetting that!"

There are things to recall, to bring back for your soul's mulching; there are also things to release to the winds—burdens or

---

blights that are contaminating your progress.

I never used corporal punishment as a parent, but I do remember physically yanking our 11-year-old son from a tree in the woods behind our house when I wanted him to go to school against his will. Years later, I apologized to him, saying: "I'm very sorry for treating you that way!" He couldn't, for the life of him, dredge up the incident. He had forgotten it. Then I could.

164
Surrender to Serendipity

"Life is what happens to you when you're making other plans."
—BETTY TALMADGE

As a child I would ransack through trash cans and hunt for useless keys to plunk in my ever-expanding collection of treasures. Instead of a key, my hands might run into a red ball, which, while hardly new, could be squeezed to build up my wrists for sports. I was looking for one prize, and I found another along the way. Serendipity struck again!

Have you ever found valuable things that have been lost by others? Have you made new friends while mingling with old ones? Have you been trafficking with an idea and, lo and behold, another one blindsides you?

Opportune things happen, if we're willing to let them. Our plans must be adjustable to allow life to do what it will with us. That's an extraordinarily rugged lesson for me as a driven, highly controlling person.

We camp for the benefit of our children but fall in love with the hobby ourselves. We search for a particular painting but come upon a gorgeous piece of furniture instead. We take an elective course, as a filler, and end up pursuing the field professionally.

I call it being pleasantly sideswiped, or as Lillian Carter phrases it: "Every time I think that I'm getting old and gradually going to the grave, something else happens."

After the death of Rabbi Moshe of Kobryn, one of his disciples was asked, "What was the most important for your teacher?" The disciple thought for a moment and replied, "Whatever he happened to be doing at the moment."

165
Taking the Fifth Fully

"Those surplus mothers spoiled us on the sly and
never got a single rose on Mother's Day."
—Elva Kremenliev

I invite each of us to pay silent yet fulsome tribute to the supplemental mothers and fathers, siblings and teachers who've enriched, stabilized, and sometimes even replaced our given biological bonds. It takes an entire village to properly raise all of us—a village of folks known and unknown, embraced and unrecognized.

Good mothers, of any stripe or locale, are those willing to touch where our hurt is, give the hurt a name, and point us in the direction of healing. And they're willing to get down on the floor and frolic with us as well.

Taking the fifth commandment seriously means honoring your father and mother. Yet sometimes our parents aren't exemplary or useful with respect to healthy honoring, so, go ahead, broaden the spirit of the fifth commandment to read: Honor any and all those adults who truly nurture and swell your horizons!

166
There's Typically Another Move

"The path leads on. The path has many steps and the
next one is always the hardest we shall ever know."
—Christmas Humphreys

There's a painting somewhere in a European gallery of the scene in which Faust sits opposite the Devil at a chess table. Faust's face is contorted in anguish, for he retains on the board but a knight and a king, and the king is in check. Thousands of people have walked by this painting, aware that in the very next move, the Devil will secure the victory.

One day a chess master happened by to stop and stare. The minutes changed to hours, but still the master stared. Then suddenly, "It's a lie!" he screamed. "The king and the knight have another move! They have another move!"

So do you and I.

167
"Faithful Are the Wounds of a Friend."
—Proverbs 27:6

Friends salute our virtues and call us on our faults, and through it all, accept us for who we truly are. The Germanic root of friend (*ber-frij*) means: this is a "place of high safety."

Every one of us has fair-weather pals who wouldn't dream of going tiger hunting, even when prodded to do so. There are also so-called buddies who have a yen to parent or coddle us, showing up when we're most needy. They just can't wait to try out their latest messianic ploy on us.

Those two types are half-friends. Sometimes they are just who we want. But most of the time, we covet full-fledged friends. We desire a handful of individuals who are ambidextrous, able to comfort and confront with equal aplomb.

Let's give special thanks for the faithful wounders in our lives. They are extraordinary gifts indeed.

168
Become a Resultist

Bishop McConnell of the Iowa Conference of the Methodist Church received a letter from one of his rural congregations that said they were being subverted by a horde of Holy Rollers. The group joined the congregation and brought in a bale of hay, threw it all on the floor, and began to roll around in fits of ecstasy.

The parish was upset by all this folderol and wanted the Bishop to kick them out of the church. The Bishop wired back: "All I want to know is when they get up from rolling around on the floor, are they better partners, better parents, and better citizens? If they are, let me know, and I'll send a shipment of hay to every one of my congregations!"

Moral results always trump spiritual rituals.

169
"People Are More Fun than Anybody."
—DOROTHY PARKER

Puzzles are fun, so are objects, challenges, and animals. But people are the most fun of all. Not always pleasant fun, since humans also generate the most pain, but over the long haul, people create the funniest and most fun-filled times available on earth.

People per se are zany, but the decisive benefit is that we get to share the fun stuff with one another. Fun alone is never quite as cool as fun shared.

Be funny and foolish today. And multiply some fun with the crazy cast of characters around you. Serious fun, playful fun, foolhardy fun, and spontaneous fun. Any kind of fun will do.

170
Believe the Future In!

"My interest is in the future because I'm going to spend the rest of my life there."
—CHRIS KETTERING

Robert Frost was once interviewed by a newspaper reporter and asked if he believed our nation had much of a future. The poet replied, "My friend, our founding foreparents didn't believe in the future; they believed the future in!"

There's a distinct difference between passive believing and active believing. The former gives lip service to this statement or that conviction. The latter is vigorous, bolstering claims with conduct.

We need to get a running start on the future. We have to prepare for it, lay the groundwork so that our tomorrows will rise from the foundations of our present. There will be surprises and setbacks, but we must always believe and act beyond the current evidence and the present moment.

Visionaries aren't snooty or snide. They're simply dreamers with a strong work ethic.

171
Join the Brigade of Galumphers!

This over-the-top word is borrowed from the author Lewis Carroll, combining *gallop* and *triumphant* and depicting whenever we creatures bound about uninhibitedly and in mercurial fashion. You and I are inclined to conduct lives of sheer structure and routine. Our todays too frequently resemble our yesterdays. Our paths are void of flair and ingenuity. We could use a little oomph and galumph!

To be sure, we can't galumph all the time or we'd run out of gas, but to do so intermittently is the mark of an exuberant, on-fire, and high-spirited soul. What spurs you to galumph about during your days and nights? Your examples may prove useful to others who are aspiring galumphers.

"There Is No Lost Good."
—Dorothy Day

In Jewish literature there are many tales about the struggles of the *zaddikim*. This term is usually translated as "the righteous" but actually means "those who have stood the test." The *zaddikim* were set apart not because of position or reputation so much as because they wrestled, day in and day out, with evil in pursuit of the good and emerged scathed but with their characters intact.

We can become cynical as we age. We condemn the messiness of politics. We downgrade the educational system. We rail against immorality. On the contrary, religion reminds us that "there is no lost good." Every moment we've spent in compassion, every cent contributed to justice, and every effort given to peace reaps dividends.

Most of our spiritual maturation doesn't happen overnight. Salvation is usually a gradual process. But never minimize any word we utter or feat we perform. Everything we say or do counts. Words and acts can save lives.

I ran into a man who lives on the edges, economically and socially, but seems to maintain sufficient stability through following what he calls his H.O.P.E. mantra: "Healthy Options Planned Everyday." Following this attitude of hope will help Steve not only for a few weeks but presumably over the long-haul. He was an authentic "goodfinder": that is, someone on the relentless quest to locate and spread the good in the unlikeliest of people and situations.

Same with the *zaddikim*, for whom goodness wasn't a passing fancy but a life-calling.

"Knowledge Puffeth Up."

Some people become insufferable because of the constant habit of show-boating their knowledge. They may know less or more than others about a given subject, but it matters not. All they care about is telegraphing their smarts. In such cases we're reminded of Paul's apt and piercing phrase: "knowledge puffeth up" (I Cor. 8:1).

Knowledge need not lead to arrogance and unctuous boasting. It won't, if it's used to enhance life rather than extend ego. For me, knowledge is more important than ignorance or credulity, but it isn't a virtue per se. Knowledge only becomes wisdom or a bona fide virtue when it's employed in service of justice and love.

Our world covets the cultivated minds of everyone committed to the pursuit of boundless wisdom. Remember the claim of Emerson: "When two people are thinking alike, one of them isn't thinking." No two of us are duplicates. We each feel, think, and act in distinct ways. You and I may share similar but never identical convictions.

Clearly, we're on earth to swap notes, learn from our neighbor, rather than wallow in smugness. But our conversations should never devolve into conversion, where one of us sways the other into thinking exactly what we think. Instead, as we delve into the differences, we discover the truly exciting subtleties of each of us, and we keep on growing and graduating all the way home.

And, by the way, no two rabbits or two waterways are the same either.

174
Keep the Gift Moving

"Love is not to be paid back; it is to be passed on."
—HERBERT TARR

We are all recipients of gifts, ones at birth and others acquired throughout our history. Being timid or grudging about utilizing our gifts is a sure-fire way to be personally unfulfilled and socially inept. Be our gifts emotional or financial, intellectual or spiritual, our chief mission during our earthly existence is "to keep the gift moving"…indeed, our gifts moving.

Our colleague Mary Harrington, suffering from Lou Gehrig's disease, kept saying to herself during her last days: "What is the most loving thing I can do now, since every day is a chance to love one thing hard." Here was Mary, in the throes of her own terminal suffering, conscious of passing her gift of love on to those who surrounded her. May we go forth and do likewise.

175
Life Is Ultimately a Gambol

"You can call it jogging if you want; you can call it tennis if you want, I call it gym. And I don't have to go anymore, so I don't!"
—FRAN LEBOWITZ

I'm told that of all the known animal species, the human appears unique in its capacity to continue play into adulthood. An insect rarely plays; mammals and birds play hard as youngsters but lose their bouncy edge in the later years. We adult humans can play right up to death, indeed play with death itself.

But, frankly, how playful are we stress-ridden, hard-driving moderns? I'm afraid not very. Like the chimpanzees, we play zestfully as little ones yet taper off our sense of zaniness as we reach maturity. All too often, upon reaching adulthood, we give up our so-called foolish ways, considering play to be a frivolous, even irresponsible luxury. Why? Because there's always work to be done, volunteer committees to staff, and letters to be written to congressional reps.

There's little room or time leftover for parades and balloons, games and idle chatter. We humorless crusaders forge ahead, unwilling, perhaps no longer able, to laugh and dance as long as there's evil and suffering in the world, which is to say we're not likely to be free enough to play much in the very near future.

Yet daily life without a sufficient dose of fun is a puny and shriveled life indeed. Human animals are here on earth to work and play in alternating rhythm, to engage in both business and monkey business, as my tennis partner loves to say.

Pablo Casals, in his elder years, got up every morning to play the piano, not to flaunt his prowess, although his musical gifts were enormous, not merely to keep physically active and mentally sharp, although that was part of this ritual too. Most importantly, I believe Casals played and we play every day, because we play to live, or is it live to play? It doesn't matter.

Play is our first act, and, if we're blessed, it will be our last one as well.

176

Actualize Your God-given Power

"Do the thing and you shall have the power.
But they who do not the thing have not the power."
—RALPH WALDO EMERSON

The German word *kraft* means power or strength. Power is resident in every one of us; yet when untapped, it dissipates and human beings wither. Power is the application of intelligence and courage to force. It must be crafted. A river may furnish a terrific force, but it develops power only when directed through a turbine.

To actualize our god-given power, then, is the basic charge delivered to everyone at birth. Consequently, the gravest human tragedy is not that we die, but that we fail to employ our full selves while wandering this single, beloved earth.

Sometimes we're just too frightened to unleash the power each of us possesses. That goes for institutions as well as for individuals.

177

Truth Is a Tricky, Twisting Adventure

Truth not only comes to us in small segments but can also be downright confounding. I saw a cartoon in the *New Yorker* created around the idea that if you could sit monkeys in front of typewriters and let them type long enough, eventually, just by chance, one of them would type the whole Bible or the complete works of British author J. K. Rowling.

So, the cartoon pictured this monkey seated in front of a typewriter, clicking away, and what you read over the monkey's shoulder on the typewriter paper is: "To be or not to be, that is the gazorninplotz!" Well, you can't have everything.

Our trek after a particular truth seems flawless. Everything is perfectly set up, and, lo and behold, we end up with part insight and part obfuscation, just like the monkeys. We're about to cradle a kernel of the truth, yet we produce "to be or not to be, that is the gazorninplotz."

The pursuit of the whole truth is a tricky, twisting endeavor not meant for brittle minds or flabby souls.

178
Paying Our Rent

"Do you know any really generous people who aren't happy?"
—Jack Kornfield

Archibald MacLeish's play *J. B.* says: "we got the earth for nothing." The gracious response then is to give back to the blessed creation everything we have and are, all the way home, and count not the cost. Put similarly, Alice Walker remarked: "The service we render is the rent we pay for our room on this earth."

Our generosity begins with enjoying ourselves, then spreading the overflow. Generosity isn't an attempt to repay the creation in full. That's impossible. We are munificent, because our cup is full and demonstrated gratitude is the best way we know how to be alive and alove.

The longer I walk this earth, the more I realize that generosity underwrites all the other virtues. Without generosity, one loves sparingly; without generosity, one acts for justice infrequently; without generosity, one hides out or hordes; without generosity, one grows stingy of gift and time and soul.

Generous people are generative people, plus they're seldom lonely. To boot, generous people experience the gratification of seeing wrongs battled, prejudices countered, sadnesses lightened, institutions upheld, while they're still alive.

Flatly put, generous people know that in the end, we possess nothing except what we've chosen to share or give away.

179
"Everyone Is a Genius at Least Once a Year."

"Everyone is a genius at least once a year.
The real geniuses simply have their bright ideas closer together."
—GEORGE C. LICHTENBERG

We need to be patient, for we are likely, at any moment, to turn brilliant. Also, the conviction that "everyone is a genius" helps us be more receptive to the insights of others. The flipside of this claim is also worth noting: "Everyone is ignorant, only on different subjects" (Will Rogers).

The second sentence reminds us that "real geniuses" tend to pack more wisdom, back to back, than the rest of us. Creative power usually is due not only to innate ability but also to remarkable perseverance. Geniuses seem to keep on keeping on. They resemble that weighted, egg-shaped toy in the shopping mall called a "weeble," an entity that shakes and shivers, even wobbles, but fails to topple over.

180
Weave Threads Not Chains

"Chains do not hold a marriage together. It is threads, hundreds of tiny threads, which sew people together through the years."
—SIMONE SIGNORET

This lesson is pertinent not only to our primary partnerships but also to every encounter, every job, and every aspiration we cherish. Chains create bondage rather than compassionate and constructive ties.

Conversely, threads—and remember tons of them, not a meager few—can weave a tapestry of exquisite beauty and strength. And even when either our clothes or our bonds turn a bit shabby or stale–threadbare–I still recommend weaving threads over chains at every turn in our trek.

181
Repair the Brokenness of the World

In Jewish lore, at the origins of life, abundant divine light was contained in vessels. However, when the vessels were broken, then discord and confusion burgeoned throughout the universe.

Hence, the task for all humans was made explicit: we're expected to repair the ancient vessels, gather the scattered light, and reconvene all who are lost. In short, our job is to repair the brokenness of the world. This process is called *tikkun*.

What a welcome and worthwhile mission it is to be designated healers and repairers of the world. Every day we awake, we know unerringly what our primary task is. And it's not a frivolous or paltry assignment; it's holy work indeed.

182
Lift and Lean

"There are two kinds of people on earth:
the people who lift and the people who lean."
—ELLA WHEELER WILCOX

There is surely a time to lift as well as a time to lean in the robust life. The trick remains knowing which to do, when, and with whom. Some of us are likely to do a lot of lifting this or that cause, this or that person. We're compulsive do-gooders. But watch out, servants can wear out if not regularly replenished.

I invite those of us who are inveterate lifters—who serve, support, and save constantly—to undertake a change-of-pace: daring to lean, let down, and welcome bolstering from beyond ourselves.

Then for those times when we need to stop leaning, I encourage us to reach down and lift up an idea, a person, or an issue.

Lift and lean in rhythmic measure.

183
Examine the Giraffe

"It is only by risking ourselves from one hour
to another that we live at all."
—WILLIAM JAMES

A friend of mine gave me a pamphlet entitled *The Giraffe Society* that honors people who stick their necks out and defy the spread of mediocrity and indifference. Would that everyone one of us would be a risk-taking individual who dares to make positive contributions toward bettering our world! Then we'd either all belong to the Giraffe Society or there wouldn't even be a need for such an organization.

Why do we need more giraffes? Because giraffes stand out above the crowd and because they're endangered by the insensitivities of humankind. Plus, they are calm and peace-loving creatures.

And, I almost forgot, giraffes can also eat and digest thorns.

184
May You Never Rest in Peace...on Earth

"Twenty years from now you will be more disappointed by the things you didn't do than by the ones you did do. So throw off the bowlines, sail away from the safe harbor, and catch the trade winds in your sails. Explore, dream, discover."
—MARK TWAIN

One newsperson asked, undoubtedly seeking an original twirl on a stale pretzel: "What words would you want inscribed on your tombstone?" Daniel Berrigan replied, gnawing the pretzel: "May I never rest in peace."

Social servants like Berrigan seldom, if ever, find complete rest for their weary bodies and disturbed consciences. Even in graves, their examples stir others to keep the faith or sustain agitating.

I remember my college roommate writing a one-act play about a holy person who chose hell over heaven because of the social service opportunities available in the former. The point of the drama was that heaven might prove too idyllic for a caring heart. The play was entitled: "Going to Hell," because that's where human misery needed to be addressed rather than being "blissed out" in pursuit of never-ending sweetness and light.

185
Gladden the Hearts of Others

"Life is short and we have not too much time for gladdening the hearts of those who are traveling the dark way with us.
Oh, be swift to love! Make haste to be kind."
—Henri Amiel

Not only is life short, so is each day. We need to think of vigorously showing kindness on a 24-hour basis. A lot of people "eat, drink and be merry," for time is fleeting. Such hedonism is rampant in modern culture. We could use more commitment to Amiel's philosophy of "gladdening." Ironically, one true way to gladden our own hearts is by doing the same for others.

186
Be Sure to Organize Goodness

"Five of you shall chase a hundred, and a hundred
of you shall chase ten thousand."
—Leviticus 26:8

We live in an era of presumed self-sufficiency. Some people believe that by banding together, their power of influence will somehow be diminished. Others baldly argue that clans are superfluous. Buddhist ecofeminist Joanna Macy reminds us: "there are two primary reasons for communities: first, we won't be alone when it comes time for us to die; and, second, it provides a place where we can speak our truths."

The ancient Hebrews also realized the importance of sharing crises and multiplying joys. Since evil is often organized, so too must goodness be. We're summoned to find good, be good, and do good. But we increase the effectiveness of goodness by joining in solidarity with like-minded folks. The truth is that there may be more goodness than evil in the world, but not by much, so everyone's combined ounces are vital.

Leviticus predicts that while five of us can interact with one hundred (20 times more), a hundred of us will engage ten thousand (100 times more).

187
Engage in Healthy Hissing

There's the Buddhist story concerning a certain village whose population was being destroyed by periodic attacks of a cobra. At length, a holy woman came to the village, and the plight of the people was made known to her. Immediately, she sought out the snake to urge it to discontinue its destruction. The snake agreed to leave the villagers alone. Days passed; the villagers discovered that the snake was no longer dangerous: "The cobra does not bite any more. Something has happened to the cobra."

Almost overnight the attitude of everyone changed. The fear of the cobra disappeared, yet, in its place, there developed a daring

---

boldness. All sorts of tricks were played on the cobra. His tail was pulled, water was thrown on him, and little children threw sticks and stones at it. No direct attempt was made to take its life but only a great number of petty annoyances and cruelties, which, when added up, rendered the snake's existence increasingly perilous.

He was nearly dead when the holy woman returned. With great bitterness, the cobra implored, "I did as you commanded me; I stopped striking the villagers and now see what they have done to me. What must I do?" The holy one said in effect, "You did not obey me fully. It is true that I told you not to bite the people, but I did not tell you not to hiss at them!"

Yes, gracious grumblers and healthy hissers we must remain, all of us.

188
"I Only Have One Life to Right Wrongs."
—JACKIE ROBINSON

The meaning of history is still in the making, up for grabs, undetermined. Thus, every day you and I have another chance to retrieve history from the brink of destruction, to make this earthly realm more wondrous and loving. Not only a chance; it's our very duty to do so.

History is neither an illusion nor a circular process of nature. It's the arena where the divine and the human collaborate to produce greater justice and mercy. Don't be shoved around by history; rather dare to shape it, as Jackie Robinson did in boldly breaking down the color barrier in Major League baseball back in the 1940s.

As a teenager I heard Dr. Martin Luther King, Jr. preach in our hometown. As a young adult I marched with him from Selma to Montgomery in 1965. As a parent we watched "King" with our children. "King," the 6-hour NBC TV dramatization of the life and death of King, gave our country another look at one of the most crucial liberation periods in its history. Seldom if ever did we urge, let alone mandate, our children to watch TV with us, but we did with "King."

We wanted them to begin to catch the elusive yet crucial distinctions between the fake violence that gratuitously floods the tube and the genuine, wrenching violence produced when an oppressed people struggle for dignity.

We wanted them to know why freedom songs bring lumps to the throats and tears to the eyes of their parents. We wanted them to meet J. Edgar Hoover and the Kennedys and learn that there's a higher moral law than that of their government. We wanted them to know that mature religion stands for unceasing commitment to justice and compassion.

King wasn't their first-hand history, but it was the history of their country. It's a history that's still theirs to join or ignore.

189
Gray Gracefully

"How dare you presume that I would rather be younger?"
—GRAY PANTHER BUTTON

There's an unwritten rule that after forty it's all replay. Don't you believe it! The exemplars of aging well are countless. Consider Joshua Slocum who set out at 51 to sail around the world alone and made it three years later. And Handel was deeply in debt and struggling to recover from a stroke when he accepted at 57 a commission to write a choral work for a charitable performance—and he produced *The Messiah*. And Edith Hamilton didn't even begin her work as a mythographer until retiring from teaching at 60, and at 90, she inaugurated a series of four annual trips to Europe.

In our men's discussion group the other night, nearly 40% of the men were contemplating or eagerly pursuing new regions of self and vocation. Most all in the room were over 40 and not holding. But olders are not inevitably elders. Time per se doesn't deliver wisdom: being gnarled and tested, courageous and bold are the qualities that initiate us into the temple of maturation.

190
Stop to Be Kind

"If you stop to be kind, you must swerve often from your path."
—MARY WEBB

Stopping to be kind comprises a quiet and gentle act, but it certainly requires ample energy and adjustment. It may be sometimes unnoticeable, but always momentous. No act of kindness, however minor or modest, ever goes wasted. Our lives normally speed along without sufficient thought for those along the road who covet our kindnesses. Mercy means swerving, changing directions, and shifting plans–stopping to be kind.

One of my dear friends, Peter, was reflecting upon what he wanted me to share at the core of his memorial service, if he happened to beat me to the grave: "Tom, in my memorial service, please don't over-eulogize me but do not fail to tell those in attendance that, after they leave the service, they're required to tell at least 5 people how important they are to them as well as spend the rest of their days being kind to folks, especially strangers. In so doing, they will be honoring me." A life that moves too swiftly for moments of kindness is moving too fast.

191
Keep Going to School

A mother asked her daughter what she learned on her first day of kindergarten. "Not enough," she answered, "not enough...I've got to go back tomorrow." Whenever we feel that we've arrived as mates, with our children, or on the job, we're spiritually stunted. We might as well pack our bags and retreat into the coziness of "cave-hood."

We need to go to bed with gratitude in our souls and wake up with anticipation in our hearts. For we've just completed, then been handed, another precious day of learning and loving.

I can't wait to go back to life tomorrow; how about you?

192
"You Shall Not Covet the Possessions of Your Fellow Human Beings."
—10TH COMMANDMENT IN HEBREW SCRIPTURES

A neighbor once spotted Abraham Lincoln trying to separate two of his sons locked in a bloody-nosed battle. "What's the matter, Mr. Lincoln?" "Just what's the matter with the whole world," he answered. "I've got three walnuts, and each boy wants two." We all covet something of somebody's at sometime. Greed occurs whenever our wealth, be it small or great, goes unshared. Ravenous and greedy beings, you and I.

I know of no better antidote to the pernicious demon of covetousness than genuine self-love. Our mission is to love ourselves sufficiently that we might be free to admire without envy and respect without coveting the possession or the personhood of our neighbor.

The recipe for a happy and holy existence is to want what we have and be who we are and dwell where we're located. Or as eight-year-old Kaila Spencer puts it: "Keep your heart clean with peace. Don't get it dirty with greed. It is not too late to clean your heart up!"

193
Have a Good Mourning

"Blessed are those who mourn, for they shall be comforted."
—MATTHEW 5:4

We receive comfort as a gracious, unsolicited gift. We're reassured in myriad ways. We're consoled from unlikely sources as well as when we directly ask for it. Jesus reminds us that we can also be comforted when we dare to mourn or weep our insides out.

Our society tries to eradicate or at least smother grieving. It trains us to ignore hurt and camouflage pain. It tries to rescue us from tragedy by offering us sweet lies or panaceas. To be grief-free is to be utterly emotionless. Open-hearted people grieve when another loses a job or home, grieve when international conflicts result in bloodshed, grieve when children make stupid choices, simply grieve every day for one thing or another.

In the process of grieving, we cleanse our senses and are fortified. Catharsis can lead to comfort. Falling to pieces often produces healing. Remember, weeping isn't the only way to grieve: others of us may turn to journaling or sitting in silence, while Zorba the Greek danced on sand when his son died.

But often, too often, we choose to suppress our hurt, go stoical, and brave it through. Until we grieve openly, we're unable to receive lasting relief. The form of our grieving matters not—just dare to grieve!

194

"It Is Only Possible to Live Happily Ever After on a Day-to-Day Basis."
—Margaret Bonnano

We can plan months in advance. We can lay out a yearly life-plan, even a five-year agenda. Yet we can only tackle our agenda on a day-to-day basis.

Whether we are pregnant or suffering from a terminal illness, on a new job or facing retirement, in or out of a partnership, our happiness is reached by taking one day at a time, hour by hour, minute to minute.

Each moment is precious and to be embraced as such; we are called not to seize or simply fill time so much as fulfill it.

195

Bring Your Hard Times Stuff Too!

A friend of mine announced a hootenanny this way: "Tonight bring your hard times music, that is, music that helps you in hard times and lifts you when you're down. Maybe someone else could benefit from your hard times stuff too."

I love the familiar Joe Raposo children's song "Sing," but there's one portion that I always edit while crooning it. The song reads: "sing of good things not bad." I think we need to "sing of good things AND bad," so that's how I amend Joe's song. I don't think he would mind. I also muse about Neil Diamond's powerful "Song, Sung Blue" where we're summoned to sing about, perhaps through, our despond. Furthermore, standing in the Latvia Square is a sculpture of a mythic woman entitled "Music" with the inscription: "Life is hard...so we sing!"

I summon us all—young and old alike—to bellow via song about our shadows (what we're ashamed of) and our dragons (what we're afraid of) as well as our ecstasies (what we're thrilled about).

Everything is fair game for a song.

196

"Ripeness Is All!"
—KING LEAR

The word *ripe* is a rich and resourceful term applicable to various zones of life. Mainly it refers to a fully grown and developed creature. I ask: isn't that our human quest, to grow to a mellow, seasoned old age? At my increasing maturity, I don't even mind being considered ruddy and plump like a fully-ripened fruit, budding to my best state or flavor.

In a similar vein, I urge us to heed the wisdom of another literary giant Blake who wrote: "And we are put on earth a little space that we may learn to bear the beams of love..." Beams could either refer to rays or timber. In the former case, we are here to give birth to particles of love.

In the latter situation, we are in the construction business. Beams are long pieces of heavy, often squared, timber and it takes real strength to bear them up as we share in the construction of our earthly abode.

Whether we are birthing or carrying, we would surely concur with the savvy of Shakespeare that "ripeness is all!"

197
"Hasten Slowly!"

The Tibetan saint Milarepa exhorted us to "hasten slowly!" This wise counsel applies whether or not we're contemplating a job change, facing death, or slogging through humdrum tasks.

We earthlings yearn to reside in zones of certitude. However, to become grown-ups, at least edge toward greater maturity, we must become adept at honoring paradoxes like "hasten slowly."

A good car driver knows when to apply gas or brakes, maneuvering ahead in timely fashion.

Our enjoyment on this planet will be enhanced when we learn how to hasten slowly: to stay on purpose, forging ahead at a measured, reflective pace.

198
Steer Clear of Helpaholism

"She loved to help others. You could tell the others by their hunted look."
—Virginia Glascow

As helpers we need to take stock of our motives. When we're driven, desperate, or foster dependencies, our helping is counterproductive for all concerned. We become care-takers rather than care-givers. Sometimes we need to be *care-fronters* who tell those struggling:

"Hey, my friend, if you need a helping hand, you might wish to start by looking at the end of your arm!"

Doing for others what they can do for themselves insures their not becoming aware of their own accountability. Care-givers realize that we're but partners in our neighbor's healing process. Our job is to serve our kin not to save them. We don't possess that kind of power, plus, in so trying, we rob others of their essential dignity. Always remember: it's their life not ours!

We ministers fall prey to helpaholism both by profession and nature. I know, for I'm a recovering helpaholic. So caught up in counseling others, I lost touch with my own partner in my first marriage. Others got more than my mate did. I have also been so caught up in producing and serving others that, over the years, I've missed crucial appointments with my own soul: conspicuous evidence of helpaholism.

199
Be Wholly without Wax

In ancient Rome, unscrupulous marble dealers would cover up cracks by rubbing in wax to make them less visible. Honest dealers would sell marble without wax (*sin*, meaning without, and *ceres*, meaning wax), being utterly sincere people.

I remember the utter sincerity of the superlative baseball umpire Ron Luciano who took his craft seriously but always with a sense of humor. He said things like "umpires never win," and "I never called a balk in my life. Why? Because I didn't understand the rule." What honesty! And here's my favorite Luciano quip: "There are lot of salls and brikes that I simply have to call balls and strikes in baseball." And so it goes.

This is the right image for living a responsible life—one that is truthful and sincere—that doesn't cover over the warts and cracks in all of our beings but exhibits who we really are. We can't promise ourselves or others an unblemished record, but we can, most of the time, become sincere persons, wholly without wax.

200
"Singing Is Inner Massage..."

"Singing is inner massage: put your hand on your chest and you'll know what I mean."
—JUDY FJELL

Singing is akin to smiling, since we're far less likely to do any harm to person or property when we're singing or smiling. It's been noted that singing is such a warm and welcoming art that Vladimir Lenin (1870-1924), the Russian Communist dictator, was perturbed that music would make him soft, if he allowed it to sink into his soul. Lenin bemoaned: "I cannot listen to music too often; it makes me want to say kind, stupid things, and pat the heads of people."

You bet it does, Comrade!

201
Pursue Humbition

Ambition has to do with ascent and aspiration. Humility reflects descent and being earth-bound. When the two are married, they create what someone has coined *humbition*, a third reality that includes yet transcends them both.

Humbition denotes a state where we're grounded yet we soar. It resembles the universal tree of life in its remarkable ability to grow up and down at the same time.

Here's an illustration of humbition: the capacity to live steadfast in the present while forging your future.

Andre Kostelanetz, the great musical director, visited the celebrated painter Henri Matisse at his home on the shores of the Mediterranean. He asked Matisse, "What is the source of your inspiration? What launches you from today toward tomorrow?" "Well, I grow artichokes," replied Matisse. "Every morning I go into my garden and watch these plants. I see the play of light and shade on the leaves, and I discover new combinations of color and fantastic patterns. They inspire me. They motivate me to move from my ground toward the sky! Then I go back into the studio and paint." Spiritually fed, Matisse kept the nourishment flowing.

How does humbition function in your life? What's the equivalent of growing artichokes in your life?

202
Dwell in a State of Perennial Recovery

"The world breaks everyone; then some become strong at the broken places."
—Ernest Hemingway

There's no one alive who stands exempt from one wound or another. Some have paid more dues than others, but all share membership in the club of the wounded. We are broken people, you and I, in our bones and in our hearts. What matters is whether we become weak or strong at the broken places. Do we mend or do we flounder in disrepair?

The sobering fact is that we never fully recover from ailments, torments, and losses. I'm reminded of that truth daily, since my broken elbow of some 25 years ago remains but partially usable. We are merely situated in different stages of recovery.

Alcoholics Anonymous sagely reminds its members that no one is a fully recover*ed*, but always a recover*ing*, alcoholic.

203

Capture Your Story in One True Sentence

"Each person's life can be
summed up in one sentence,
and it should be a sentence that has an active verb."
—CLARE BOOTH LUCE

In his book *A Moveable Feast* Ernest Hemingway recalled his early years as a writer in Paris. He talked of the anguish of fellow writers who felt that they had pulled the last possible word out of their minds and guts, languishing with barren imaginations. What kept these writers going, Hemingway argued, was the conviction that if they could just write one true sentence, they could complete another story.

Sometimes it requires days, even weeks to write that one true sentence, but the effort needs to be made. Even when we don't produce the true sentence, the process stirs and enriches us, keeps us churning on course.

A true sentence means composing or constructing something that brings joy to our days. It might be an act of forgiveness or changing a habit. A true sentence is any gift that boosts both the giver and the receiver. What is your one true sentence that encapsulates your mission on earth?

And, remember, you can edit the sentence along the way, or

write new ones too, but at the close of your jaunt, I urge you to choose but one clear-cut epitaph.

204
Grip and Be Gripped by Some Passion

"You spend a good piece of your life gripping a baseball, and in the end it turns out that it was the other way around all the time."
—JIM BOUTON

That's certainly the case for me as my days of playing catch with our grandson have begun to fade. His fastball is just too much for my left hand, padded glove and all, to absorb anymore, but we still fire tennis balls to one another in swimming pools. When Petco Park opened in San Diego ten years ago, my wife, Carolyn, purchased, as a surprise, a brick placed on the promenade area of this major league baseball stadium. It would mark her partner's boundless passion for baseball.

She bought the plaque, and I chose the inscription: "Tom O-T and baseball, friends forever." Whenever my grandson and I go to a Padres game, which is often, we rub that plaque as a good luck charm. I hope he continues to rub it, long after I'm underground.

205
Grown-ups Turn into Hybrids

There is too much pigeonholing nowadays. You are a radical. She is a liberal. He is a conservative. This can either end a conversation or start a horrid debate. The reality is that we're concoctions of all three with different emphases from time to time. To be *liberal* is to be open of mind, generous of heart, and free of spirit. A *radical* goes right to the source or root of a concern. To be *conservative* means to treasure things and to hold on to what is worthwhile.

You see, at our most evolved, we can be combinations of the three. Hybrids, if you will.

206
Capitalize the Hyphen

Following a college lecture, essayist Sydney Harris was queried: "What was the greatest single advance in human knowledge?" And he replied: "It was the use of the hyphen." Nervous laughter rippled throughout the audience. But I concur. Politics and economics, justice and mercy, must be yoked in a commendable education.

When we married, we hyphenated our last names to Owen-Towle. Carolyn and I were aspiring to blend the richness and resources of both of our affectional histories rather merging them into one. The hyphen was a bridge and balancer. As Carolyn later mused: "We would capitalize the hyphen in our name if we could!"

207
"I Am Lovable and Capable!"

I started off my ministry, some 45 years ago now, working primarily in religious education with children and youth, and our bedrock mantra for nurturing the soul and healing the world was IALAC, which stood for *I Am Lovable and Capable*. Often when things weren't going so well, either for individuals or classes, we would revisit the IALAC poster on the wall, the IALAC cards we produced for each child to carry around in their wallet or purse, and the IALAC hats we donned at certain events.

It was a constant reminder that each and every one of us had inherent potential, that we were all beautiful and cool creations, that, if we truly affirmed the core of our own dignity, we could make a difference in our daily worlds: at school, at play, and at home.

None of us should leave home without an IALAC card attached to our body or soul.

208
Welcome the Interruptions

While teaching at Notre Dame University, theologian Henri Nouwen met an older, experienced professor who had spent the bulk of his career there. While they strolled the campus, Henri sensed a certain melancholy in the voice of his companion: "You know, my whole life I've been complaining that my work was constantly interrupted, until I discovered that interruptions were largely my work."

Our streets are forever in disrepair. Children and parents are constantly bumping into one another. Interruptions are a reminder to be fully present and accountable. Don't take anything for granted. Engage and enjoy whatever emerges. Be willing to be detoured, even derailed, by graceful, even niggling, interruptions.

"As Iron Sharpens Iron, So One Person Sharpens Another."
—PROVERBS 27:17

Contrary to popular belief, good friends and resilient couples bring their toughest stuff to the relational table. They don't pussy-foot around difficult emotions; they vent them in beneficial ways. Devoted buddies neither bully nor back off; rather they come on strong. They are willing to pit their multiple strengths alongside rather than against the other. Result: everybody involved emerges both sharpened and sharper than in their separate existences.

Here's the way a friend of mine, Mary, boldly phrases it about her husband of 17 years: "Sinewy of body, dogged by a low pain threshold, Bert's keen mind and emotional verve drew me to him and keep drawing me to him. In Bert's own way, he is steely and iron-like, and I have felt encouraged to display my emotional and moral muscle next to his in our partnership."

Mary and Bert are "as iron sharpens iron."

Be Thankful for Mountains and Valleys

"For overhead there is always the strange radiance of the mountains."
—D. H. LAWRENCE

One of the reasons we returned to California, after living some years in the Midwest, was to move amidst and beneath not just mounds and hills but hefty mountains. Upon reentry into our home state, I remember the surge of enthusiasm upon attempting to climb Mt. Whitney. I wasn't particularly interested in conquering, only in befriending, it. I hoped to uncover fresh feelings about rock, ice, wind, animals, sky, and self, something of what the wise of old meant by "refreshment of spirit."

Having reached Trail Camp, I sat down, rested, ate, and then I shored up my body for the final ascent up this tallest of mountains in the continental United States. As I looked up and beheld Mt. Whitney, an incredible rush of sentiment swept through me.

I experienced overpowering awe and a sense of littleness before the implacable grandeur of this majestic mountain. Part foe, part friend, it was glaring at me, daring me. I felt afraid yet energized.

I climbed to the top.

Many of the spiritual giants of history have made similar treks up mountains, reaping inspiration and facing temptations. The temptations, while less noticeable than the benefits, must also be saluted. There's the temptation to eternalize joy, to stay "high" all the time. Or the enticement to hide out in the wilderness, turn ascetic, withdraw from the complications of social life, then morph into a mountain muse. Jesus told us to reject such temptations. He invited us to visit the peaks but live in the plains. The visions received on the mountain must be served in the valleys of ordinariness.

I headed back down the mountain. Upon reaching our base camp, I crawled into my tent, exhausted and proud, and gave thanks for both mountains and valleys.

211
Every Being Is Irreplaceable

Knowing that he was about to die, Auguste Comte (1798-1857), the French philosopher and pioneer in modern sociology, murmured out loud: "Oh, what an irreparable loss!" On the one hand, Comte's claim sounds egotistical, and it might be better if someone else had proffered those words about him than Comte himself. Yet it's a lot better than saying: "When I die, there promises to be no detectable loss."

No one is indispensable; there is always someone available to fill our role. But we are each irreplaceable; for no person walks the earth with precisely our same gift and gait. In the Talmud, the rabbis queried why God began with *one* being instead of *hundreds*. Answer: because the Infinite Spirit wanted to demonstrate that every creature is singular, fresh, and unprecedented.

If we've been reasonably proud of our earthly jaunt, then we can confidently, not cockily, announce, upon our impending death: "It will be an irreparable loss" when I am gone. Yes, it will.

212
Our Hands Have Jelly on Them!

Charlie Brown is eating a peanut butter and jelly sandwich. He looks admiringly at his hand and says: "Hands are fascinating things. I like my hands. I think I have nice hands. My hands seem to have a lot of character. These are hands that may someday accomplish great things...They may build mighty bridges or heal the sick or hit homeruns or write soul-stirring novels (Charlie is yelling by now). These are hands that may someday change the course of human destiny!"

Lucy looks down at Charlie's hands and says: "They've got jelly on them!"

Lucy's right, our hands have jelly on them; but they are all we have. Jelly or not, flawed and messy, we're going to have to keep on using them to make meanings in our universe, even if we never really "change the course of human destiny!"

213
Your Pudding Needs a Theme

The story goes that Winston Churchill was dining one night at a deluxe restaurant. After a scrumptious repast, the British Prime Minister ordered pudding to crown the evening. Churchill found it displeasing and hailed a waiter to his table: "My good sir, the pudding is interesting but clearly lacks a theme!" Such is the plight of too many moderns: our lives lack any discernible theme, let alone a fulfilling one.

My openly-declared bias is that loving and being loved constitute the governing themes of our individual and communal journeys. Only love, at its truest, can transform lives; only love can redeem civilization.

"Jesus Is Full of Surprises"

"Whoever feels attracted to Jesus cannot adequately explain why. We must be prepared to be always correcting our image of Jesus for we will never exhaust what there is to know. Jesus is full of surprises."
—ADOLPH HOLL

Based upon 90 sayings verifiably attributed to Jesus, according to the measured verdict of the "Jesus Seminar" of contemporary biblical scholars, I agree with these somewhat surprising claims:

- Jesus didn't consider himself a messiah nor did he send his disciples out to evangelize the world. This was essentially the marketing venture of the early Christian Church.
- Jesus seldom mentions God and harbors no particular doctrine of God. He was spiritually akin to Buddha or Socrates, figures more concerned with ethics than metaphysics, holy pilgrims who spoke in parables and paradoxes, occasionally illuminating issues, but frequently leaving us swimming in confusion.
- Jesus recommended celebrating over either prayer or fasting, regularly cavorting with sinners and prostitutes, indiscriminate in his eating and drinking habits, a veritable party-hound.
- Jesus was "a powerful social deviant" in that women accompanied him publicly; furthermore, he treated children as full human beings.
- Jesus was scathing in his criticism of the self-righteous and believed that "awards were always intrinsic" and that "love is its own reward."

Whether we're religious conservatives or progressives, there's no way to tailor or tame Jesus into one of our like-minded spiritual buddies, for he was tirelessly challenging the smugness, corruption, and pedantry of all religious types, including you and me. Jesus remains chock-full of surprises and not always ones we would consider agreeable.

215
"Be Good to One Another or Else!"

One summer we heard the poet-songwriter Rod McKuen speak in Oakland, California about his new book entitled *Finding My Father*. It was a telling tribute to the tenacity of forging bonds. He autographed it for us, penning these words: "To Tom and Carolyn, be good to one another or else!" Ominous and pointed, yet shrewd, advice.

Marriages where mutual good will doesn't reign supreme eventually crumble. Unilateral affection or trust doesn't do the job. There may be personal needs or fantasies, but partnership demands nothing less than a relationship, and a relationship only exists where there is mutuality. There's no such thing as a one-sided relationship.

In a mature, ever-evolving partnership basic questions ache to be answered: Is there something nourishing that I can do today to deepen our committed bond, and, moreover, am I willing to do it again tomorrow, even when I might not receive kudos for it?

I have a cartoon that depicts a couple standing at the local Marriage Recorder's office and asking plaintively: "Do you have any ceremony less drastic than marriage?" Not really. In fact, married or not, if you choose to pursue a committed bond between parent and child or adult to adult, mutuality is always required.

Sobering news, isn't it?

216
Judge Not

"Judge not, that you be not judged. Why do you see the speck that is in your neighbor's eye but do not notice the log that is in your own eye?"
—MATTHEW 7:1, 3

We are prone to miss our own poverties of character and swift to note those of our neighbors. We do this not from confidence but insecurity. However, if we spend a good deal of time criticizing and damning, there isn't a whole lot of energy left with which to love mercy, be kind, and do justice.

Branches or shingles, specks or logs, the size of the wood isn't at issue. The real concern of this biblical admonition is to urge us to spend our moments cleaning up our own house rather than gawking at the messes in the abodes of others. You may need to shape up your body and enlarge your heart, but my homework assignment is to labor on my own condition not yours.

Anne McCaffrey's line holds me in fine stead: "Make no judgments where you have no compassion."

217
"Thou Shall Not Kill"

Life is our most precious earthly possession. But when this noble and sweeping commandment is put in absolute form, "thou shall not kill," we find it impossible to heed. For life feeds on life; it exists only by the destruction of life. We cannot help but kill to live.

So we try narrowing the scope of the commandment: thou shall not kill persons. Put thus, it reflects our deepest ethical impulse, and yet there may be instances where the refusal to ever kill persons can lead to vastly greater hurt and destruction.

No trouble-free rule. On the one hand, the iron necessity of nature: life kills to live and, on the other hand, the human commandment: "thou shall not kill." So, here's where I end up. There's an essential sanctity that attaches to life, to all life, including animal and plant life, and it's right to violate that sanctity only when the failure to violate it would lead to violence even more grave.

Granted, sometimes I must do what injures life; therefore, let me dedicate myself never to injure life except in the necessary interest of life. And let me, as I value life, come humbly to every choice I make, be it concerning abortion, animals, capital punishment, euthanasia, or warfare....recognizing that none of my choices are pure and clean. Furthermore, may we be vigilant not just about killing the body but about destroying the mind and spirit within others as well as within our selves.

In sum, our mission is to comply with the ancient Jain doctrine of "ahimsa" that means dynamic harmlessness. Ahimsa renounces the will to hurt any living being through hostile thought, word, or deed, but, furthermore it includes the conscious integration of compassion into our daily lives.

The spirit of *ahimsa* is based on the unitive quality of life found in the cooperative structure of the atom; the symbiotic relationship among the plants, soil and air; the social quality among human beings and other species of animals; and in the magnetic forces that maintain the balance of the solar system.

Nothing is more crucial in today's global reality than humans aspiring to embody *ahimsa*.

218
Be Truly Religious

"We sometimes have just enough religion to make us hate
but not enough to make us love one another."
—JONATHAN SWIFT

To be sure, horrendous things have been done in the name of a rigid, ruthless version of religion. On the other hand, the right dosage of an open, caring faith can heal wounds and activate moral change. The etymology of the word "religion" promotes positivity.

First, *religare* means "to bind together again." The words "ligaments" and "loyalty" are kin. As a religious people, we bind ourselves to the primary realities of existence: self, neighbor, nature, and God. Furthermore, the *re* denotes our doing it repeatedly. In an era of division and rupture, religion is a vital bridging, healing, and binding endeavor. Healthy religion is more a matter of compassion than judgment, recalling that in the Christian scriptures alone, 20% of the texts demonstrate Jesus healing folks and only 1% center upon rules and regulations.

Second, religion comes to us from *religere* meaning "to gather together again." We're not sufficient unto ourselves. The religious person visits but dwells not in solitariness.

In sum, the authentic religious life is one where we gather together to participate in the life of binding with all that is truly important, over and over again.

Listen

"If it is language that makes us human,
one half of language is to listen."
—JACOB

I recently noticed that silent *and* listen have the very same letters; the only difference is the way those letters are arranged. No surprise, since listening and being silent are accomplices in fostering communion.

Have you ever noticed that when Michelangelo did the Sistine Chapel, he painted both the major and the minor prophets? You can even tell them apart because, though there are cherubim at the ears of all, only the major prophets are listening.

Yes, we speak too much, too frequently, too impulsively, and often bemoan the result. Healthier relationships leave lots unsaid. They know when and how to hold tongues, leave verbal crossfire to talk shows, and just button up. As Diogenes wrote: "We have two ears and only one tongue in order that we may hear more and speak less."`

Communication demands an ample supply of both speaking and listening. The art of hearing seems more difficult to sustain. That's why we grew two ears instead of one. To be a good, responsive listener is to be about as passive as a good surgeon. Steady, reflective, and quiet but hardly passive.

Listen to the speech of others, even more to their silences. Go deeper. Listen to the subtle sounds of their beings. Silence can exist without speech, but speech cannot live without silence.

And a Teenager Shall Lead Us

Our oldest child, Chris, now 51 years old, shared something beautiful and precious about "love" way back on his 13th birthday. He penned:

> *Love is a powerful meaning, and when the powerful meaning is used toward another person it will raise that person eternally.*

Note the verb "used." You see, finally, love to be itself must be a verb. It only exists in action. Our younger daughter was so taken by her older brother's wisdom that, for awhile, she had it taped to her bathroom mirror.

I pay close heed to the third chapter of the Rule of St. Benedict which states: "When anything important is brewing, you call the community together and listen for the spirit. And you pay close attention to the youngest, the least experienced member to speak first, so they won't be overwhelmed by the experts."

This doesn't mean that we glorify children or youth per se or that we always end up following the counsel of the greenest person in the room, but it remains sound practice to listen to any voice that is relatively fresh, less powerful, and unencumbered with accrued prejudices.

Maintain All Your Marvels!

"We have scrubbed the world clean of magic."
—ALAN WATTS

Something catches us off guard, leaves our mind spinning and heart throbbing. It's magical. However, if not careful, one can get lost in the esoteric or abstruse. Magic is harmful if it diminishes our sense of objectivity. At its best magic opens us to wonder, keeps us playful, and alerts us to portions of life that remain beyond our figuring and control.

Ten years ago I took up magic to bring a sense of wow into my life, to make sure that I kept "all my marvels" during the home-stretch. It's been a kick becoming a silly senior or a wily wizard as well as combating arthritis, maintaining mental acuity and motor skills, and sharing moments of watchable wonderment with all ages. As I've ventured into this strikingly new craft, I've learned that it's alright to have butterflies in the stomach, just as long as I teach them to fly in proper formation—at any rate, some of the time.

222
Mediocrity Is Tempting

"Only mediocre persons are always at their best."
—Somerset Maugham

We are all mediocre in one thing or another. The challenge is to combat the tantalizing trap of being mediocre in most everything. Mediocrity is tempting, because it costs all we have to be a person of excellence; it's hard, a lifetime effort. If we want to be safe and secure, then mediocrity is the place to stay.

There's the story of the chair of the pulpit committee who was being painfully honest: "We don't want someone who's either too liberal or too conservative. We just want someone who's mediocre!" This faux pas illustrates the plight faced by any group selecting leadership—be it in business, education, religion, or politics. The danger is clear: we try so hard to avoid extremes that we sometimes settle for mediocrity.

The most creative, vibrant leaders in society aren't wobblers, waiting to see which way the wind blows. They risk taking strong, even controversial, stands.

223
"The Trick Is to Use the Mess..."

"The trick is to use the mess, to make the messy things work for you."
—JOHN IRVING

We are prone to cover or clean up messes, our own as well as those of others. A death occurs; we repress rather than express our deepest feelings. Our work situation sours, so we blame it on job conditions instead of scrutinizing our own efforts.

Most of what really matters in life is messy. We would be amazed how often elements of our messes can become assets and work for us, if employed in quest of some imaginative order.

224
Never Stop Wishing

President Dwight David Eisenhower reminisced about growing up in Kansas. Once he went fishing with a pal, and the two young boys pondered what they wanted to become when they grew up. "A major league baseball player like Honus Wagner" was Eisenhower's wish. His buddy said: I want to become the President of the United States." Well, Ike reflected later on, "It looks like neither of us got our wish!"

In truth, our early wishes seldom materialize, for they're often either unreasonable or unachievable. So we need to keep on wishing, since there might just be a magnificent dream waiting to be realized...by you and you alone.

225
Obey the Requirements of Micah

"And what does the Lord require of you but to do justice, and to love kindness, and to walk humbly with your God?"
—MICAH 6:8

Three telling requirements from the book of Micah.

First, do justice, don't just think about, visualize, or applaud it. As the poet William Stafford reminds: "Justice will take millions of intricate moves."

Second, love kindness. When in doubt, be kind. When furious, be kind. When vengeful, be kind.

Third, walk humbly with your God. Not the gods of someone else but your very own interpretation of God: a Being worthy of your particular service and company. And while walking, do so with a sense of humility.

From my perspective, there's no finer summary of life's objective than this passage from Micah.

Give Three Cheers for Life's Mistakes and Cracks

"I make mistakes, and I'll be the second to admit it!"
—JEAN KERR

Musicians make mistakes; good ones weave the mistakes into meaningful spurts of joy. Ballplayers make mistakes, and theirs even show up in daily box scores.

In a religious education classroom in Providence, Rhode Island, an imaginative teacher created the phrase: "nobody gets to be wrong" in this classroom. To be sure, there are times when we're inaccurate or bad, every last one of us.

Nonetheless, her point holds. We make mistakes, but we aren't mistakes. Furthermore, those kids who are considered to be "pains" can change. And this teacher's environment assists the little ones in growing into positive, beautiful, caring young persons, despite their mistakes.

Here's another image on the related theme of cracks, composed by the poet and songwriter, Leonard Cohen:

Ring the bells that can still ring
Forget your perfect offering.
There is a crack in everything.
That's how the light gets in.

Ponder for a moment the dazzling, glorious light that hankers to break through the cracks in everything and everyone.

"Things Take Time."

"Put up in a place where it's easy to see the cryptic admonishment T.T.T.
When you feel how slowly you climb, it's well to remember that
Things Take Time."
—Piet Hein

The Danish cartoonist Piet Hein has produced books full of what he called "grooks," such as the one above. Things do take time. There's no trickier art to master than patience and waiting. Ponder the places in your life that exhort you to be patient, that take ample time. Remember: not only things or tasks take time, so do people and so do solid relationships. I believe in evolution; how about you?

There's a different twist to this grook. Things take time, people take time, work takes time, TV takes time, meditation takes time… there are many experiences in our lives clamoring for our limited moments. Which are consuming the bulk of your time? Never forget that you are in charge of who or what fills the time slots on your schedule.

And how about the story of Gutzon Borglum, the sculptor who created the tremendous Mount Rushmore Memorial? Borglum was once asked if he considered his work perfect in detail. "Not today," Gutzon replied, "because the nose of George Washington is perhaps an inch too long. It's better that way, though, since it will erode to be exactly right in approximately 10,000 years."

Yes, T.T.T.

228
Move Beyond Categorical Thinking

"The narrow-minded ask, 'Are these people strangers,
or are they members of our tribe?' But to those in whom
love dwells, the whole world is but one family."
—HINDU SCRIPTURES

We do altogether too much classifying in life, eagerly categorizing individuals—in and out, good and bad, right and wrong, conservative and liberal. An evolved religious path affirms distinctions, but it doesn't let them block the quest for unity and harmony.

It is often said that on most every issue the world can be divided into two kinds or people: those who divide the world into two kinds of people *and* those who don't. I urge us to reside in the second category, but I guess even that statement fosters the classification mentality we yearn to shirk.

229
Money Is Liquid Power

"Money is better than poverty, if only for financial reasons."
—WOODY ALLEN

There's the story of the robber who ambles up to comedian Jack Benny, sticks a gun in his ribs, and says: "Your money or your life!" Benny pauses awhile and replies: "I'm thinking, I'm thinking!"

Few of us are that tight with our cash. However, there still lurks in the crevices of many a mind the erroneous and destructive notion that money and life are opposites. You keep one, you lose the other. That simply isn't the case. Money and life are profoundly linked. Money is liquid power, granting muscle to our visions, energy to our values, and reality to our commitments. In short, money can bring life. As someone asked, "What does *Amen* mean?" The answer, "I'm for it, and I'll stand my share of the expenses."

Ironically, Jesus talked about money in 16 out of 38 parables, and 1 of every 10 verses in the Christian gospels is related to money and possessions, so obviously the Nazarene thought it important and had little difficulty speaking about it.

You and I live beholden to many beautiful visions that need our full-fledged support. We owe them our time, talent, and treasure. We owe them our money. We owe them our life.

Your money or your life? Both, my friend; both is the answer.

230
It Helps to Be Prepared

"Scholars tell us that James Madison, the father of the United States Constitution, was a man totally devoid of charisma.
He was not handsome, articulate, or charming.
He, however, had one overwhelming asset:
he was always prepared."
—John Taylor

As a Boy Scout it was drummed into us via both our stated oath and our leaders to "be prepared" under all circumstances. It was good counsel, but I had no concept of the scope of its relevance until I went off to college, followed by seminary training, then entered my first ministry, and am now settling into retirement. Preparation may not be one of the primal virtues in life; but it qualifies as one of the top instrumental values. Preparation enables all sorts of good stuff to be actualized.

Distinguish Between Principles and Tastes

"In matters of principle, stand like a rock.
In matters of taste, swim with the current."
—THOMAS JEFFERSON

This is sound counsel for befuddled parents trying to do right by our children. We often mix up principles and tastes in nurturing our offspring. I've learned, the hard way, to offer my own principles and display my own tastes to let our children know who I am and what I prefer. Then I back off, allowing both of us to amble ahead.

My parents, on the whole, were pretty good teachers. They knew how to be both firm and flexible in relating to my brother and me. Styles, fashions, tastes, and opinions would come and go and weren't, from their perch, worth going to the barricades. Yet values, meanings, and principles weren't budgeable matters as far as Mom and Dad were concerned.

Professor W. E. Hocking would always contend that we cannot have a sound society unless we always have a sufficient number of people who cannot be bought. He called them "the unpurchasable ones." These are women and men who not only stand by their principles through thick and thin but also consistently act upon them. My parents, on the whole, were such kind of folks.

They weren't picky about this habit or that peculiarity of mine, be it in the area of food, clothes, or hobbies. On the other hand, they stood strong and unyielding on concerns of friendship, academic excellence, honesty, and compassion. Their own lives

---

banked on those values, and they wanted their sons to bank on them as well.

Harold and Mary, my models.

232
Shirk Any Monument in Your Name

"After I'm dead, I'd rather have people ask why I have no monument than why I have one."
—Cato

In Wolfgang Amadeus Mozart's 35 years of life he never garnered a particular prize. There was no evidence of a trophy case in his den. The gifted and graceful creators of humanity have been transported to greatness more by interior vision than external carrots. We're an "over-trophied" civilization. Awards are ours almost for the asking. Due to ingratiating kindness we distribute ribbons for all entrants. This is sincerely done, for there is merit in democratization. I know firsthand as our son's Cub Scout Master years back, since I gave a prize to every Cub Scout in our pack who chose to enter our Pinewood Derby contest! My decision understandably rattled the cage of some of the more goal-oriented fathers.

However, something is lost in the relative ease with which we erect memorials for our living and dead. We begin to idolize shrines rather than admire persons. What if we quit constructing monuments altogether and spent commensurate energy and effort studying, then following, the lives of those humans we wish to honor?

233
"Joy Comes in the Morning."

"There may be tears during the night, but joy comes in the morning."
—PSALM 30:5

Every night when we retire, my wife, Carolyn, and I try to oust whatever frustrations and angers we might have accrued during the day with ourselves, work, one another, or whatever. This ritual cleanses us for sounder sleep.

However, there still remain nights when we're unable to quiet either one of our spirits. Our sleep is punctuated by fears and tears, unease and upset. Even occasional nightmares. We restlessly wait for a new day, high in the hope that joy will sprout with the sun.

"Foreplay "–spiritual and physical–truly launches in the morning!

234
Nothing Dies When Remembered

Following the death of a fellow parish member we would engage in a Sunday morning ritual (usually preceding a formal memorial service), concluding with these words: "We extinguish our flaming chalice to mark Suzanne's physical death, yet the memories of her special character and singular conduct continue on in our lives. Her beautiful spirit is indomitable. We now light a candle to symbolize her influence that endures. In mystery we are born, in mystery we live, and in mystery we die."

Did you know that the Hebrew phrase for *dying* translates as "being gathered unto one's people?" All of us hanker, don't we, upon death, to be gathered unto our chosen people: our partnerships, our friends, our families, and our faith community? All of us yearn to be remembered. For the opposite isn't merely being forgotten but potentially being dis-membered, torn asunder, cast off, and lost.

Nothing dies when remembered. If we remember and are remembered, life endures, meaning reigns, and hope perseveres.

235
Survey Life Squarely with a Moral Squint

"If you could just see the facts flat on, without that horrible moral squint, with just a little common sense, you could have been a statesperson."
—ROBERT BOLT

Life may be less complicated but certainly shallower whenever we fall prey to expedience rather than view matters with a moral squint. Ethical gadflies are necessary to insure that the honest and honorable aspects of every private and public issue are saluted. How will this transaction generate more good for more people than before? Is this deal fair and just? Will this benefit our children's children? Are we, as inhabitants of the earth, pleased with how we are treating it?

These are all questions born of a moral squint.

236
Let's Hear It for Mortality

"A sense of mortality should make us smarter. Life is short, so you do your work. You spend more time attending to music and art and literature and less time arguing politics. You plant trees. You cook spaghetti sauce. You talk to children. You don't let your life be eaten by salespeople and evangelists and the circuses of the media."
—GARRISON KEILLOR

The Psalmist writes: "so teach us to number our days that we may apply our hearts unto wisdom." Yes, our days are numbered. Each one is precious, a gift not to be frittered away but spent, resourcefully and lovingly, all the way to our final rest, our singular death.

I resonate with the African saying that when someone is dead, "their feet are in agreement, for they have ceased moving." Being alive means staying in motion, ample emotion, even commotion.

237
Turn Up the Quiet

"People should take a few minutes a day just to empty, to become extremely quiet. Whether you consider it meditation, relaxation, deep quiet or prayer doesn't make any difference. The brain is allowed to enter into deeper states; there's much more to you when you come back."
—JEAN HOUSTON

We will probably choose, on any given day, to accomplish at least one thing we truly enjoy. We always find time for the "must" jobs too. We may even set aside moments for accomplishing a radically new or different task.

However, most of us will do everything imaginable to circumvent quietude. We're too busy filling up when we need to empty out. Exercising, while crucial, isn't what I mean. Neither are naps. We need moments of plain, unadorned, unremitting stillness.

Talking per se is of no particular value. "A word spoken in due season," as Proverbs suggests, is what truly counts: the right word at the right time in the right place. As they say, the health of any vital partnership is often measured by the number of teeth marks in your tongue.

There's an unwritten law in Vermont that people are not to speak unless they are certain that what they have to say will be an improvement upon the silence. That's the rule of Quaker worship too.

Generally, we live in a culture where it would behoove us all to "turn up the quiet!"

238
Bury One Regret Per Week

"Regret is an appalling waste of energy; you can't build on it; it's only good for wallowing in."
—KATHERINE MANSFIELD

Admittedly, we all possess regrets with respect to lost loves or lousy jobs, things we've said or done, left unsaid or undone. No one stands clean. We all wear cuts and scars that chafe.

The mandate, however, remains: every day, certainly as we age, we would do well to bury a regret or two. Various ways exist to do this: we can journal them into oblivion; we can release them via bellowing in a safe corner of the backyard; or we can confess them prayerfully to another or to ourselves.

Be fearless enough to get rid of your persistent regrets and resentments, before they get rid of you.

A friend of mine, when she was dying, wanted to clean her slate, so she called an antagonist to her bed and said: "I want to end by being your friend once again; I refuse to go out with a grudge. What do you say?"

Both dissolved in tears.

239
Keep Mulling Things Over

In the House of Commons, British Prime Minister Disraeli made a brilliant speech on the spur of the moment. That night a friend said to him: "I must tell you how much I enjoyed your extemporaneous talk. It's been on my mind all day." "Well," confessed Disraeli, "that extemporaneous talk has been on my mind for 20 years!"

Bright folks aren't just insightful on the fly; they've been composting, not just composing—mulching their material, over and over, for years. I remember sitting daily with my father-in-law as he laid-in a painting or brought one to completion, sometimes sitting with him for hours. It was a pure delight being in the presence of an artistic genius.

One day I was emboldened to ask: "How long, Millard, does it take you to start, then complete a painting?" and he sagely answered, "70 years, Tom, 70 years," implying that it took all he could muster for the duration of his entire life to produce any specific work of art.

240
Small Isn't Always Beautiful

"Some people can compress the most words into the smallest ideas."
—ABRAHAM LINCOLN

We live in an era imbued with E. P. Schumacher's keen concept of "small is beautiful." This is an understandable rejoinder to times when bigness in everything reigned supreme. However, there's a shadow side to smallness.

Three people are frequently too few for effective group discussion. Folks with small hearts are unable or unwilling to give much. And, as Lincoln warned, small ideas, especially when wrapped in showy verbiage, are useless. Beware of any slick slogan or phrase you're tempted to post on your refrigerator or the bumper of your car.

241
Create Your Very Own Music

"All the music is out there in the first place, all of it. From the beginning of time, the music was there. All you have to do is try to get a little piece of it. I don't care how great you are, you only get a little piece of it."
—DIZZY GILLESPIE

There's the story of the great violinist Jascha Heifetz who was booked for a concert in a large U.S. city. The weather was horrendous, and only six people showed up. So, Heifetz said to his audience: "Friends, forget my concert, let's go to a smaller room, have a drink and just talk about music." And one of those present quickly rose to his feet and exclaimed: "No, Jascha, no! I've come hundreds of miles just for this evening's concert. Come on, Jascha, sing something!"

People are mistaking what we do all the time. They have an erroneous notion of who we are. It doesn't really matter as long as we chuckle at the misperception, keep on making our own kind of music, and get on with our lives.

One caution remains: whatever you do, don't die with your peculiar piece of music still lodged within your soul.

242
Life Is Mainly a Game of Names Not Numbers

In the Genesis narrative naming is one of the first things done. God names humans, then invites us to name the rest of the animals. Life is off and running.

Our names are shorthand for the fact that you and I mean something special. An Irish-American mother, when told by a priest that the name she had chosen for her daughter was not a saint's name, replied, "Not yet, not yet." Holy or not, each of us is unrepeatable and unravels a distinct identity.

Our first name is ours to play with during life. Our middle ones are intriguing links. Our last name bonds us with a lengthy, affectional heritage. Some of us have constructed new "handles," bidding farewell to our given ones. I've had the privilege of celebrating such renaming ceremonies.

I will regularly open a retreat of young adults by having us analyze our names: how we got them, what they mean to us, and where they might have either carried or failed us. This has proven to be a vitalizing, often intimate, exercise. We close with a ritual wherein each of us slowly states our full name out loud three times.

I've found it to be strangely true that whenever we speak our own name or hear the name of another spoken with respect, even reverence…all manner of harm (whether within or beyond the room) is significantly diminished.

243

Tinker and Tweak Only When Necessary

Falkland, a martyr of the English Civil War, as he stood facing Hampden and Pym, said: "Mr. Speaker, when it is not necessary to change, it is necessary not to change." Or as the folk wisdom runs: "if something ain't broke, don't fix it!"

Perpetual meddlers have tended to tinker with this relationship or that machine. We can't leave well enough alone. We're dissatisfied with how we look, where we work, and what we achieve. Tinker, tweak, tinker, tweak…all the way home.

Sometimes it's desirable to stay unchanged.

244

Negatives Block Us

"Nothing clutters the soul more than remorse, resentment, and recrimination. Negative feelings occupy a fearsome amount of space in the mind, blocking our perceptions and pleasures."
—NORMAN COUSINS

There is understandably a place for creative protest and occasional naysaying. Indeed, in the *Upanishads*, the Hindu holy book, we are urged to engage in the art of pruning, saying "neti, neti": not this, not that…on the road toward producing any optimal result.

Negative feelings can't be ignored or denied; they must be faced internally, then released in good time, in appropriate ways. They need to be harvested. Yet Cousins is concerned, and so am I, about folks stewing in their own negative juices: unresolved rage, lingering bitterness, or extended grief. Such emotional states are guaranteed joy-blockers.

245
It All Comes Back to Personal Pluck

"My dear thing, it all comes back, as everything always does, simply to personal pluck. It's only a question, no matter when or where, of having enough."
—HENRY JAMES

We can be bright, we can be well-intentioned, we can concoct a masterful life-plan, but without pluck we will travel only so far. Pluck is that indescribable "oomph" that shows up in our daring, nervy deeds.

Here's an inspirational story of pluck drawn from the world of music. In 1995, the brilliant concert violinist Itzhak Perlman was performing at the Lincoln Center in New York City. During the midst of his performance, strings on his violin suddenly burst, leaving Perlman with merely three strings. He refused to stop, but plowed ahead: shifting, recomposing, and noticeably altering the classic piece.

Perlman "plucked" his way to the finish, basking in thunderous applause from a stunned yet appreciative audience. Then, without boasting, Perlman offered this pearl of wisdom: "Well, you know, sometimes your job is to find out how much music you can still make with what you have left!"

Such is life's challenge: getting music out of life's remainders after the break has come; winning the battle with what is left from a defeat; going blind, like John Milton, and writing sublime poetry or deaf like Beethoven, and composing superb sonatas.

Nothing is quite as impressive as personal pluck.

246
Locate the Spiritual Path that Fits You

"God chooses one person with a shout, another with a song, and yet another with a whisper."
—RABBI NAHMAN OF BRATISLAV

In today's marketplace, gurus are a dime a dozen, especially spiritual ones. I'm all for guides, but gurus make me jumpy. Those who speak in definitive tones are more promoters than teachers. I prefer companions over charlatans.

My version of religion declares that there isn't one pathway to spiritual fulfillment or serenity. There's a welter of potential routes. God steers us through various means, and we return the favor with our own versions of the Infinite. Through trial and error we land upon a spiritual discipline satisfying our temperament and desires.

And there's no need to get unduly bothered, since any conceivable practice will be flawed and flabby, just as we are.

247
Follow the Philosophy of "Nevertheless"

When Henrik Ibsen, the Norwegian dramatist, came to die, his last word was "Nevertheless." He was a great critic of the society in which he lived, so how fitting that this should be his final term: "Nevertheless."

Here are other examples of the philosophy of "Nevertheless."

- Let us forge ahead unitedly to mount this campaign–nevertheless remain sensitive to the caution of those who strongly disagree with our plan.
- She was unsure she made the right decision to leave the job–nevertheless she chose to live well with this decision.
- I quarrel with my country–nevertheless I love it.
- Life can prove difficult, even dreadful, sometimes–nevertheless it's good to be alive.

248
Volunteer Your Services

Here are some of the ostensible reasons why I spend time, during my retirement, playing the guitar, singing, and chatting during the lunch hour (called "Social Dining Time") at a nearby nursing and rehabilitation center.

- When I was a youngster, around 10 or so, my hand went up when our local minister asked if any of us were willing to accompany him on visits to the private as well as institutional settings of some "old-timers" in our church. My peers thought me strange, and I probably was, but I had grown up, from two years old on, with one of my grandmothers living in our house (after my grandfather committed suicide), so infirm seniors were not a foreign, let alone distasteful, experience for me. Actually, spending time with elders eventually became one of the prime reasons I felt called to become a minister as an early teen.

- I still feel one of our premier human challenges is to spend quality time seeing those who are invisible, hearing those who are unable to say much, and touching those who are perceived to be among the "untouchables" of American society. All three types of people are noticeably plentiful in nursing homes.
- And, yes, my mother spent her final two weeks in a nursing home, and whenever I engage a resident at the local Balboa Nursing and Rehabilitation Center, I am mystically reconnecting with her.

All I know is that when I leave my hour of sharing with these kinfolk, there is a fresh lift and lilt to my life. Is there a comparable call or challenge in your current life where you volunteer your services and therewith feed your soul? The place to start is where your personal passion matches a specific global yelp. Pick a place or task that speaks both to your heart and to the world. Then, as the ad puts it: "Just do it!"

249
Run On...Walk On

For several years I engaged in a bunch of 10Ks, chugging along the best my body and heart would allow. One of my pacemakers or inspirers was named Howard. He was a chatty guy, who would engage me in light conversation to moderate the slow-driving pain of jogging the 6.2 miles. During one run, Howard unpacked his remarkable story. Twelve years back, he had been 250 pounds, on drugs, and essentially homeless. Slowly but surely, Howard had negotiated an implausible comeback, thanks to being in recovery plus tons of loving support from buddies combined with a rigorous regimen of running.

Howard had run some dozen marathons in the intervening years and totally turned his life around. As his story continued, I fell silent, tears falling down my cheeks; then he said farewell and sped ahead to finish yet another race. At the end I couldn't find him, but Howard had indeed paced me physically for a short while but spiritually for a much longer stretch.

I didn't see Howard for years; then I ran into him at the gym where he was walking on a treadmill, still moving, moving more slowly but moving ahead. There were no more runs left in his body, but Howard remained "my pacemaker."

Never forget that when the disciple asks: "What is absolute truth?" The master simply answers: "Walk on, walk on, walk on, walk on!"

250
Pack Your Bags for the Final Passage

When Pope John XXIII lay dying, he was asked if everything was as satisfactory as it could be considering the circumstances. The Pope smiled and said: "All my bags are packed!"

People whose lives are fulfilled have their spiritual houses in order. They've separated the wheat from the chaff. They only track possibilities within their limits. They neither overrate nor undergrade their gifts. They continue to serve others. They don't postpone living. If they can sing or dance, they do so constantly; if not, they certainly bounce and skip some every day. And through it all, they refuse to banish their smile.

They are prepared for their private date with death.

251
Become Whole Not Perfect

"You, therefore, must be perfect, as God is perfect."
—MATTHEW 5:48

The word *teleios* in Greek doesn't mean perfection or incapable of error, but translates as wholeness, fully realized, completion. Too often, religion demands the frantic, vain pursuit of perfection. We clobber ourselves, as well as others, by engaging in such an elusive quest. The truth is that perfection of any kind is impossible anywhere, whereas improvement of every kind is feasible everywhere.

Our aspiration should be to become whole persons whose bodies, minds, and spirits are coordinated: individuals, who, recognizing our blemishes and flaws, attempt to integrate them into our lives. Three cheers for our faults, minor and major, those we've already shown and those, to quote Pogo, "we haven't even used yet." We only fail if, once and for all, we throw in the spiritual towel and cease caring.

In the first of the two creation myths in Genesis, at the end of each, God sees what was created and says, "Tov" or good. After six days, when Creation is complete, the Eternal One says "tov nov" or very good. If perfect isn't possible for God, then it isn't for any of us earthlings.

252
Make Room for Paradoxes

*"I learned to make my mind large, as the universe is large,
so that there is room for paradoxes."*
—MAXINE KINGSTON

The Hebrew scriptures are saturated with ambiguities. For starters, with regard to the subject of war and peace, pacifism is supported in Micah 4:3 and Isaiah 2:4, where "they shall beat their swords into plowshares and their spears into pruning hooks." Yet those who prefer militarism can find biblical support for their position in Joel 3:9-10 where the command is to "beat your plowshares into swords and your pruning hooks into spears." Faced with opposite views on practically every subject, with variant grades in between, rational folks have been quick to dismiss the Hebrew scriptures as literature of competing contradictions, and therefore, irrelevant.

But I ask you: is not life itself full of niggling opposites? Do not, in fact, paradoxes constitute the setting for our daily meandering? For example, whenever I pick up my tennis racquet and take to the court, tennis is surely as Billie Jean King notes: "a perfect combo of virulent action in an atmosphere of tranquility." Enumerate a few of the paradoxes you ride during your days and nights as a pilgrim.

253
Keep It Simple, Stupid!

You're probably familiar with the KISS rule: "keep it simple, stupid!"

There's the story of James Bevel, the civil rights activist, who said that the trouble with average preachers is that "they speak about mendacity and prevarication, and you still don't know whether or not they're against lying!" His moral: don't use big, confusing words when you want folks to be stirred to take a stand!

And there was the misprint in a newspaper story that recorded that the preacher's upcoming text would be: "Though I speak with the tongues of humans and of angels and have not *clarity*, it profiteth me nothing." One only hopes that the minister read this blurb prior to their sermon.

Here's another illustration depicting absolute verbal confusion. A woman came up to Adlai Stevenson after a speech in Chicago and said; "Oh, Mr. Stevenson, you were absolutely *superfluous* today!" And he said, "Well, thank you, Madam!" Then she went on to say: "And I hope you publish those remarks that you made today." And Stevenson replied, "Well, Madam, in view of what you said, perhaps I should publish them posthumously." "Oh, yes," she retorted, "and the sooner the better!"

Our job is to communicate, both as speaker and as listener, using the proper words of the proper size, making connection and being understood. Be simple without being simplistic; in short, "KISS."

254
We Are Renewable Creatures

"I feel that as long as the earth can make a spring every year, I can!"
—ALICE WALKER

Sometimes when we're weary or drooping, our necessary energy boost will arrive not so much from human kin but rather from the sprouting and blossoming of the natural world. The sun is rising some place in the world right now, and something is blooming somewhere.

We often bank utterly on the light of those around us. Ours is flickering; we need the boost of their illumination. Nonetheless, when pressed, we would be amazed at the amount of juice we can generate by ourselves when we are despairing and unenlightened. There are unimaginable sources of light available in the depths of our beings, waiting to be used. We need to let the lights of our inner beings burn as brightly as possible before requesting outside assistance.

Life is renewable. And so are we.

255
Meet the Love of Your Life

"Do you want to meet the love of your life? Look in the mirror."
—Byron Katie

When we round into our seventies we finally come to comprehend that while the world can't give us true peace and happiness—since we can only brew them in our own hearts—by the same token, the world can't take them away. My mission statement in essence is this: nourish the self with healthy nutrients then spread the nourishment abroad.

We need to hold on to the unique body and mind we were bequeathed and are now growing. By hold on, I don't mean squeeze or cling, but hold lightly and openly, so that our being can breathe and expand. You and I are our own possessions, actually the only ones we will ultimately take to the grave. As the Zen Buddhist koan states: "I can only nod to myself!"

The sincere practice of self-possession provides life's launching pad.

A Good Parent Resembles a Sturdy Moccasin

"Making the decision to have a child is momentous. It is to decide forever to have your heart go walking outside your body."
—ELIZABETH STONE

The ups and downs of the average parenting career are astounding. There isn't a parent alive who doesn't seriously question at one time or another, "Why did we get into this racket in the first place?" And, of course, there are countless adults who have no business birthing offspring. They are undoubtedly fine folks, but they aren't equipped for parenting.

Just when things are going beautifully, an unexpected trauma occurs, and it doesn't matter whether our child is at fault. A trauma is a trauma. As someone quipped, "a parent is neither cocky nor proud, because they know the school principal may call at any minute to report that some child, perhaps theirs, has just driven a motorcycle through the gymnasium." Parents need to be resilient, roll with the punches, stand armed with ample fortitude, and quit watching, as Florida Scott Maxwell bemoans, "for signs of improvement in their middle-aged children."

Good parenting doesn't mean being an idyllic, even ideal, parent, which isn't likely. It isn't even having your child turn out well; for that all depends on countless factors, especially upon their choices not yours.

This may seem like a strange analogy, but, frankly, a good parent resembles a sturdy moccasin: warm and soft on the inside, yet firm and strong without. Good parenting is essentially about staying loving, staying flexible yet stout, and staying the course.

257
Peace-and-Earth Are Interchangeable

"It is in each of us that the peace of the world is cast…in the frontiers of our hearts, from there it must spread out to the limits of the universe."
—CARDINAL SUENENS

In Russian, the word for peace is exactly the same as the word for earth. When the Soviets say "Peace on Earth," the terms are interchangeable. We start with ourselves, ousting, as much as possible, the warlike symptoms residing in our own souls. Then we spread "peace-earth" outward from there.

Our understanding of peace must be as expansive as the size of the globe. A peace that is pursued within the confines of our own hearts is puny. A peace that extends to our family and friends, but no farther, isn't large enough. We are placed on earth to bring peace to the entire planet.

It helps to heed the Aramaic translation of "peacemaking," which means "planting peace every season." And being a genuine *peacemaker* is a far more demanding quest than merely being *peaceable*–accommodating, sweet, and nice.

This much is certain: if you truly aspire to be a peace-maker, not merely a peace-seeker, you will never be out of work.

258

Thank Your Teachers

*"Each gave me something for my journey: a phrase, a wink,
an enigma, and I was able to continue."*
—ELIE WIESEL

There have been teachers who nudged and yanked me further along my path. I don't cite only classroom conductors. I also allude to neighbors, coaches, relatives, ministers, and peers without whom my journey would have been less instructive and inspirational. They awakened me from slumber. And, by the way, our teachers can be either mentors or tormenters; it matters not.

Without such companions, I might not have continued the trip. In any case, they certainly made my jaunt more meaningful.

When teachers are asked the question, states analyst Ronald Stephens, "What makes a great teacher?" they tend to answer: "Knowledge of subject matter." On the other hand, when students are asked the same question, they usually answer with four qualities: "Patience, understanding, the ability to communicate, and love." In short, students aren't that impressed with how much a teacher knows, but they're deeply concerned about how much a teacher cares about them.

How do you feel about your teachers over the years? Are there special ones who showed more interest in you than in the subject matter? And have you thanked them either in person or in thought?

259

"Perseverance Is Many Short Races One after Another."
—WALTER ELLIOT

A marathon is composed of more than four ten-kilometer races. A 10K race is made up of several shorter jaunts. Good runners break up long races into measurable units. They run certain times for each mile. They sometimes even stumble or fall down, but they clamber back up and stay on course.

Goal setters work in terms of specific and achievable challenges rather than tackling one gigantic, usually insurmountable, problem. Or, as my buddy suggests: our biggest problems need to be addressed, maybe even solved, when they are small ones.

Break life down into bite-size, doable tasks; you're more likely to be satisfied.

260

Be Cautious around Pieces of Truth

The devil once went for a walk with a buddy. They saw a woman up ahead stoop down and seize something from the ground. "What did that woman find?" asked the friend. "A piece of Truth," retorted the Devil. "Doesn't that disturb you?" "No it doesn't," replied the devil, "since I shall allow her to make a complete religious tenet out of it."

Here's what happens when we tenaciously grasp but a swatch of wisdom. We expand, often glorify, it. The piece then becomes a precious opinion that often hardens into a bias, perhaps a religious dogma, and we willingly exclude or wound others in its name.

261
Polish a Single Gem Until It Shines

"If thy eye is single, the whole of thy body will be lit up."
—MATTHEW 6:22

Sometimes we can't seem to focus on any specific direction or we're apparently at odds with everybody. Then, due to internal and external sparks, our lives stabilize. When our lives are "lit up," ablaze with meaning and intent, our eyes are focused, and we know what we want to do and are ready and willing to accomplish it.

Singleness of mind and vision is a great motivator. The Buddhists call it *samadhi*, or doing something wholeheartedly: when we eat, we eat; when we reason, we reason; and when we serve, we serve.

Check out the foremost social activists and spiritual communicators of history: they harbored a singleness of conviction. They didn't jump from cause to cause but answered a single, unifying call. They took one gem like love or justice or mercy and polished it until it shone.

262
Obey the Platinum Rule

Most of us are quite familiar with the Golden Rule, discoverable in every world religion: "Do unto others as you would have them do unto you." But, as someone conveyed to me recently, most folks in the modern world need to outgrow this glaring focus upon "me, myself, and I," and conscientiously honor the differences in folks everywhere. This means spending more time practicing what is called the Platinum Rule: "Do unto others as *they* would like to be treated!"

The Platinum Rule requires getting to know your neighbors as they actually are, not as you imagine or project them to be. Try it: the results can prove stunningly beneficial for all parties.

263
Plodders Make Advances, Sprinters Make Dust

Great composers don't set to work because they are inspired but usually become inspired because they're working. Beethoven and Mozart settled down day after day to the job at hand much as an accountant settles down each day to her figures. They didn't waste time waiting around for a mystical experience. They persevered. They perspired. They weren't frenetic; they were just hardnosed plodders.

One great artist once said, after she had been working for 18 years on a landscape, "well, the sky is finally getting interesting!"

If we want a better society, we work at it, we plod. If we want a more loving relationship, we work at it, we plod. If we want to create something beautiful, at least interesting, we work at it. We plod.

Life Is Incurably Yin-Yang

We soon learn that everywhere in life there exists a balancing of opposites: contrasting yet complementary forces, indispensable to each other and observable in every situation. For example, the eleventh poem of the *Tao Te Ching* records: "What gives the clay cup its value is the empty space its walls create." You see, a cup is both substance and space. These opposing forces are designated by the categories of yin and yang.

Hence, the yin-yang symbol is made up of two inverted tear-drop shapes, one dark and one light, which together form a full circle. Each half is depicted as partaking of the other. Every thought, feeling, or circumstance has something of its opposite contained within it: nothing is pure or absolute in and of itself. It's impossible to cut the yin-yang circle in half (with a straight line) without having part of each opposite on both sides. The ramifications of this truth are enormous!

Think of the work station, every primary relationship, the parenting enterprise, as well as our bedrock beliefs: are they not, all of them, riddled with creative tension, in short, living paradoxes? All life is in process, and that process is a balancing of equally valid and opposite stresses.

Daily we tend to opt for either a yin or a yang. As the cheerleader in the cartoon yells out: "Give me a yin; give me a yang!" or as my tennis buddy puts it more crudely: "There's a yin and yang to every thang!"

"It Is Never Too Late to Give Up Our Prejudices."
—HENRY DAVID THOREAU

We play favorites from the moment we emerge from the womb. As babies we establish primary connections with those nearest and dearest in our empire. We're wary of outsiders and uneasy with strange things.

As we grow up, the challenge is to avoid the hardened mind-set of estrangement. Differences are to be tolerated, even appreciated, but when they are sources of alienation, prejudices are born. Some prejudices are modest, others more pronounced, even pernicious.

I know of a father whose daughter is a lesbian. He was a rigid homophobe and became visibly distraught, even scornful, upon his daughter's declaration. In fact, he couldn't communicate with her for months. But, as his daughter's next birthday drew nigh, he grew a change of heart. The father took his daughter out to lunch followed by a long walk in the woods. Then he tearfully bubbled over: "Susan, I've come to realize that I could either love my prejudice *or* love you, but there wasn't room in my heart for both. And, although it's been a painful journey, I've come to realize that my love for you is greater than my love of any prejudice. You are my daughter. You are who you are. I will not forfeit my love for the continuance of a prejudice."

It doesn't always work out in such a positive manner, as we all know. Some of our prejudices are never removed. But others can be dumped.

If possible, dare to say farewell to one callous or cruel prejudice today. The size doesn't matter.

266
We Are the Sum of Our Gifts

In Antoine de St. Exupery's book *Flight to Arras,* he wrote: "A country or a farm is not the sum of its parts; it is the sum of its gifts." He was indicating that the true significance of anything lies in the totality of its commitments. Our families will only be as strong as the number of gifts contributed to the whole by the various members: gifts of time, talent, and truthfulness. The same holds for religious communities and worldwide ventures.

The authentic nature of our beings is revealed by the depth and range of our gift-giving. We're placed on earth to give generously and unceasingly of our riches and resources.

At the end, we will be nothing more and nothing less than the sum of our gifts.

267
"Thou Shall Not Steal"

This commandment rests on the belief that property is a kind of extension of the owner's self. Therefore, acts of theft are violations of personhood. That's why, on a communal scale, mature morality requires us to construct economic systems where everybody can share equitably in life, liberty, and the pursuit of happiness. This commandment has to do with caring for the weakest and most exploited members of our human race.

In addition to issues of economic justice, the eighth commandment prompts us to halt the spiritual, intellectual, and emotional robberies we commit daily. We all, at one time or another, participate in the stealing of time, of ideas, and of space. We must monitor and minimize the pillage and theft we commit intentionally and unintentionally in all zones of our lives.

And, perhaps most importantly, this commandment reminds us that the possessive instinct has its limits. There are realities that cannot be owned, only enjoyed. The countless wonders of nature and human affection lie in the category of being unpossessable: love and stars, stones and oceans.

268
Sidestep Procrastination

"Don't put off until tomorrow what you can put off until the day after tomorrow just as easily."
—MARK TWAIN

There's a time to ponder matters, even postpone them. We all have a "wait until later" drawer, folder, or basket on our desk. Some things just need to gestate or bubble. They will be dealt with at a more propitious moment.

Nevertheless, some of us slide into bad habits, even ruts. "Putting things off" becomes a way of "doing" life. Procrastination can take up many of our waking hours. We figure out inventive, sneaky ways to keep from doing things that must be faced. Procrastination is more than a noxious habit. It can become a full-fledged malaise, if left unattended. Of course, that's part of the double bind for the procrastinator, isn't it? The person puts off doing anything about his or her procrastination, thus aggravating the problem.

I think procrastinators should list the payoffs they get in stalling and postponing, then see if they can obtain similar dividends in other more favorable ways. They might be surprised.

Lest I come down too hard on procrastinators, I confess to suffering from the opposite problem: I can be obsessive-compulsive about dates and tasks.

269
Be Both a Creator and a Protestor

Albert Schweitzer recalled the time that he chided Casals, the militant and outspoken social idealist, for his strident, controversial public utterances. Schweitzer told Casals that it might be better to create than to protest. "No," replied Casals, "there exist times when the only creative thing we can do is to protest. We must refuse to accept or acknowledge what is evil or wicked."

In truth, creating and protesting ought to be mates in concocting our calendars. We would be prudent to become ambidextrous, comfortable in wielding both. It's no longer sufficient for the disenchanted to engage in nonstop protest. These folks need to spend time producing worthwhile options too (remembering that protest literally comes from *pro-testari*, meaning "to testify on behalf of"). Conversely, some people can become ivory-tower creators, generating beautiful artifacts, but essentially disappearing when the call goes out to oppose evil.

Create and protest, protest and create all our days and nights.

270

Repent Today

In the Midrash you're encouraged to "repent one day before you die!" "But I won't know when that is!" "Yes, that's the point; repent now!"

There's a story from the Christian scriptures that illustrates full-bore repentance. A man cleans out his home, flushing it of all the available demons. Having done a thorough job, he then takes off on a trip. Upon his return, the house is filled with new demons and "the last state of that man becomes worse than the first." (Matthew 12: 43-45)

The problem is clear. This person has rid his life of previous bad habits but has failed to put anything useful or nourishing in their place. Eliminating the negatives is crucial but only a first step. We must bring in some positives to fill the vacuum.

Repentance requires denouncing and announcing. We need both to eradicate evils as well as furnish goods in order to produce a full-fledged change. To repent means literally "to turn around" —not just negotiate a little twist or a modest tweak, but actually navigate a change of direction.

What relationship or burden clamors for repentance in our lives? And are we brave and bold enough to repent here and now?

271
Track the Purposeful Life

I find the wisdom of Joanna Macy quite compelling as she defines three qualities of the purposeful life. First, we're called to work with our passion on projects about which we care deeply. Second, she exhorts us to work with our pain as well as with people whose pain touches our heart. Thirdly, Macy charges us to work with what dwells right at hand, not someone next door or something next year, but the folks and facts smack dab in front of us.

During my college days we were encouraged to be "reasonable adventurers" rather than crazy or foolish ones. Macy's life-plan synchronizes nicely with my collegiate counsel.

272
Participate Only in Useful Quarrels

We run into recalcitrant folks daily: people who have obtained their opinions strictly on an emotional level and cannot be reached through rational discourse. It's better not to try and argue with such extremists. You will end up swapping invectives. Ours should be an open (not empty) mind. We change our minds too. But trying to mix at a serious level with closed minds, well, that's a futile effort.

The English essayist William Hazlitt refused to argue with people who disagreed with him. He considered it pointless, since they didn't changed their minds. Rage and frustration typically result from verbal brawls. In Grandma's famous phrase, "we might as well save our breath to cool our porridge."

However, it can prove helpful to quarrel with those already in your camp. The arguments are often fierce but fair and friendly, because you treat one another as enduring colleagues rather than opponents. We gravitate toward pallid, fawning embraces with our buddies, when it might prove valuable, upon occasion, to spar with them. Honest scraps are likely to produce worthwhile outcomes, even shifts in attitude and behavior.

As the storyteller Michael Meade says about friendly spats: "When we get together, there's always some music and laughter and usually an argument. We don't plan to squabble, it just happens due to the fears and ferocities of our deep friendship. Anything venomous that occurs is fed to the dogs afterwards."

273
Be a Risk-taker

"There are essentially four kinds of risk: the risk one must accept, the risk one can afford to take, the risk one cannot afford to take, and the risk one cannot afford not to take."
—PETER DRUCKER

I would go further. I think that everything humanly possible entails some form of risk. Even staying in bed in the morning involves certain risks: the risks of atrophying emotionally or missing out on unborn possibilities.

If life involves risk-taking, then we must ask ourselves: what risks do I select and which ones do I choose to avoid? Personally, I think the riskiest risks transpire when we stay the same.

Halford Luccock urged us to be careful of the temptation to evade or equivocate in life: "We are beset before and after by proverbs which whisper, 'watch your step.' We are told that 'discretion is the better part of valor.' And what sweet music it often is to our ears! We readily forget that the epitaph on the gravestone of many good causes has been 'died of discretion.'" Zen Buddhist masters chuckle at any of their disciples who deliberate endlessly, refusing to make up their minds. As they put it: "People who deliberate fully without ever taking a step will spend their lives on one leg."

Ponder, then act, but avoid expiring in the arms of discretion.

274
Become a Quitter

There exist plenty of times when our duty is to stop doing something, to cease and desist, to become a full-bore quitter. It might be daring, even drastic, to quit self-destructive habits such as smoking or overeating, quit a job that is going nowhere, or quit saying spiteful things to those we love.

Look deep into your soul today and select one attitude or behavior that you could well afford to quit altogether. Just do it, furtively, without either rancor or bombast. And after awhile, you may even wish to join Quitters Anonymous for ongoing support.

275
Pull Your Life Off Hold

Did you hear about the woman who believed so fervently in reincarnation that she made a will leaving everything to herself? Or the man who said: "Personally, I used to believe in reincarnation, but that was in a previous lifetime."

Such quips illustrate why reincarnation has never particularly appealed to me. I know there are those tragic births or life travesties that would seemingly justify persons returning to this planet for a start-over. Certain individuals who have endured severe hardships the first time around appear to deserve a better fate the next time.

Nonetheless, there's something quite self-serving about reincarnation. Do we not have, in most cases, ample opportunities for manifold changes during our allotted days? Can't we modify, if not transform, our bodies and spirits sufficiently during the course of one lifetime? And does not waiting for a better shot next time tend to put our present lives "on hold?"

276
Enlist As a Sentinel

Legend tells of a contest between an elephant and a thrush. The elephant boasted that he could make himself heard the farthest and dared the thrush to accept the challenge. The thrush did. Then the elephant raised his trunk and sent a forth a piercing blast. The thrush quietly sang her song. The judge went forth to find out just how far each contestant had been heard.

On and on they traveled until no one could hear the elephant's sound any longer. Yet they could still hear "ever so softly" the song of the thrush. "How could the thrush's song possibly carry farther than the elephant's cry?" asked the judges. Calmly, the little bird explained: "Well, let me tell you. Our thrush family has sentinels stationed throughout the forest and when one sings, another takes up the song, and then another and another. So we pass it along until the melody is carried throughout the land." What a privilege and duty to suit up as moral sentinels throughout the forest of existence taking up and transmitting the songs of joy and justice!

277
Always Be Respectful

Respect means "to look at something or someone again." Respect-ful persons are those who look again at what is easily ignored or missed. They look again at outworn, debilitating patterns and con-sider developing new habits. They look again at their own motives before casting judgment on others. Practitioners of respectfulness remind us to look again at the history of gender disharmony and racial brutality in order to create a world beyond it.

Authentic respect has nothing to do with aloofness or symbio-sis, arrogance or subjugation. It is instead grounded in an active gaze and level glance. Respect holds the other firmly yet freely in its sight. Respect declares: "You and I are equally worthwhile cre-ations. I hold you in the highest regard. Your time, your tasks, your needs, your visions are as significant as mine and will be treated as such in our relationship."

278
"There'll Be Plenty of Room in Eternity for Us All."
—Theodore Roethke

I have always appreciated that in the Hebrew scriptures the con-cept of *salvation* was etymologically tied to an understanding of spaciousness and breadth. Christianity reinforces the same vision: "In my Creator's mansion, there are many rooms…" My reading of both wings of the bible counters any effort to save merely my own hide at the expense of others going to hell. From my perch, excluding or damning others is bad doctrine. My mission is being an ardent advocate for the whole of creation being saved.

Universal salvation means that everyone has access to the "room in eternity." In our view, there exist enough rooms to accommodate every one. No one who wishes to come inside will ultimately be left homeless and out in the cold.

279

Occasionally Ruffle Feathers

"Do not preach smooth things."
—ISAIAH

It's easy to be glib; it's difficult to be profound. There is surely a time in every life to stroke folks or smooth things over. But there also exist plentiful occasions to ruffle feathers, where it's one's solemn duty to "raise some hell" at work or play, even at home, if that's the location of the pressing assignment.

Where in your daily trek are you summoned to wreak some creative and constructive havoc? Be ingenious: you can find abundant sites and times in which to ruffle some feathers. We all can.

280

Befriend Sadness

There's the story of the baptism of King Aengus by Saint Patrick in the middle of the fifth century. Sometime during the rite, Saint Patrick leaned on his sharp-pointed staff and inadvertently stabbed the king's foot. After the baptism was over, Saint Patrick looked

---

down at all the blood, realized what he had done, and begged the king's forgiveness. "Why did you suffer this in silence?" the Saint wanted to know. The king replied: "I thought it was part of the ritual."

Well, genuine sadness is attached to our very humanity; it's part of life's ritual. Surely, we can and must always address persistent depression or seasonal despond, but sadness per se is neither superficial nor eradicable. We can only endure it sometimes, or if blessed, we can embrace sadness.

An example. When my father died in 1987 on Christmas Eve, I knew that my own holiday memories would never be the same again. Indeed, no Christmas season arrives now without my feeling the poignant combination of expansive joy and bone-deep sadness. Unfailingly, I huddle close amid loved ones, sing lustily, and weep quietly during the dark, dank, difficult days of December.

All the way to my own grave, Decembers will be more painful and profounder, because I refuse to run from my sadness.

281
Unsullied Virtues Are Lifeless

"I don't like people who have never fallen or stumbled. Their virtue is lifeless and of little value. Life has not revealed its beauty to them."
—BORIS PASTERNAK

Honesty kept to oneself, love unexpressed, courage merely imagined, justice in the abstract—are all floating ideals. Only when risked in the skirmishes of life, only when embodied, however imperfectly or partially, do virtues emerge as authentic and full-fledged.

I appreciate the unpretentiousness as well as the humor of the following anecdote which illustrates the point of today's wake up call. There was a Trappist monastery in which the monks had taken a vow of "perpetual silence." After five years of observing the rule, a monk finally broke the silence one evening at supper to say, "I don't like the way they fix the potatoes around here." Five more years of silence elapsed, and then another monk, sitting across the table, said, "I like the way they fix potatoes around here."

Five more years went by without a word being spoken, and then a third monk said, "I can't stand all this bickering!"

The truth is that every last human being, at one time or another, has shared a sullied moment, be it an exchange of bickering, boasting, or backbiting. None of us are pure and faultless beings—never have been and never will be.

282
Turn into a Salty Creature

The most effective human beings are like salt. They often dwell in the background. You don't even notice their presence in familial or organizational work, but without their existence, there would be an appreciable loss. Their brackish seasoning would be sorely missed. Things just wouldn't taste as good. Like salt, we humans should make everything we touch more enjoyable, sometimes even transformed.

To be sure, sometimes we humans say or do too much. We overwhelm a situation or neighbor. We come across as coarse, cross, or caustic—simply too salty. So it should be noted: being a salty creature takes discernment.

283
Revisit the Full Story of Valentine

It seems improbable to link Valentine's Day with prison reform and justice until you learn the true story of Valentine, a Roman who was martyred on February 14, A.D. 270. He wrote a farewell note to the jailer's daughter who had befriended him while he was in prison, signing it, "Your Valentine."

Our concept of Valentine's Day will deepen considerably, if we're willing to visit a nearby jail to find out what actually happens to "criminals" and what can be done to humanize the penal system…as well as be willing to deliver boxes of chocolates to inmates.

It seems consistent for the fully loving soul to share a romantic exchange *and* pursue some justice at the same time.

284
"Lean into the Sharp Points"

Pema Chodron, contemporary Buddhist teacher, in most all of her writings, challenges us to face our fears rather than fight or flee them. It constitutes her foremost lesson. Along that same vein, whenever attempting difficult things, Chodron challenges us to undertake five interlinking lessons under the rubric of what she calls "leaning into life's sharp points":

- Confess your hidden faults.
- Approach what you find repulsive.
- Help those you think you cannot help.
- Anything you are attached to, let it go.
- Go to places that scare you.

Every one of these furnishes a hefty spiritual workout, so I would recommend tackling but one per month.

285
Save and Savor

"If the world were merely seductive, that would be easy. If it were merely challenging, that would be no problem. But I arise in the morning, torn between a desire to improve (or save) the world, and a desire to enjoy (or savor) the world. This makes it hard to plan the day."
—E. B. WHITE

Every day, to be fulfilling, requires a nourishing mix of saving and savoring. Our existence without compassion grows narcissistic. Our journey without joy grows martyrish.

Life's consummate obligation is to keep our balance: sharing equal moments of service and pleasure. The irony is that sometimes they turn out to be one and the same experience!

286
Keep Others Scratching

There's the story of Sojourner Truth, the slave woman who could neither read nor write but couldn't tolerate either slavery or the second-class treatment of women, so she relentlessly stood tall on behalf of equal rights for all.

Once when Sojourner Truth was addressing a crowd, a heckler tried to unnerve her: "Old woman, do you think that your talk about slavery does any good? Why I don't care any more for your talk than I do for the bite of a flea." Truth gathered herself, then retorted, "Perhaps not, but the Lord willing I'll keep you scratching!"

For Truth, being a pesky resister was neither a hobby nor a sidelight; it was her preferred way of being fully human.

287
We All Need Scut Work

I'm glad to see the phrase "scut work" finally appear in our *Webster's New World Dictionary*. It reads: "menial, routine, trivial labor." I had my share of household chores growing up, but it wasn't until women's liberation struck home that I began to appreciate the range of responsibilities or so-called "scut work" involved in being a domestic engineer.

My wife and I both have worked outside the home for most of our marriage, so we've had to share the drudgery (and artistry) involved in scut work. Much of it demeans the human spirit. Yet I confess to being glad for scut work. After being a minister who has labored daily with people over intangibles and irresolvable crises, mindless work has become a welcome respite. Cleaning toilets and dishes provides a much-needed break and change of pace. Over the years I've even become an occasional holy terror with the mop, broom, sponge, vacuum, and plunger.

Our brains and hearts seek time-outs. So, would you join me in expressing gratitude for occasional scut work?

288
Swap Questions Across the Generations

"The father sat in a garden and contemplated the grass and the tree and the bird in the tree and the small child contemplated his father. And the child asked: 'Why?' and the father smiled and said: 'I was about to ask you the same question.' And he wondered: 'Is this child as old as I am or am I as young as this child?'"
—WILLIAM BARNETT

There are definite wisdoms we parents must convey to our children before they leave the nest. There are also lessons that our children transmit to us before we die.

Then there are those treasured moments when, as Barnett indicates, adults and children turn to each other and offer up similar imponderables: "Why are we here?" "Who are we humans anyway?" "What happens after life?" And so forth. We elders may have spent more time wrestling with these queries than our younger cohorts, but we have no more unraveled the mysteries than they.

We are all wandering wonderers in the face of the secrets and glories of the universe. We serve one another well by swapping our unpretentious lessons…via letters or tweets.

289
Be Silly at Least Five Minutes a Day

"Every one is a damn fool for at least five minutes every day; wisdom consists in not exceeding the limit."
—ELBERT HUBBARD

Some of us have trouble being silly and foolish at all, let alone for five minutes every day. The world scene furnishes us with taxing, burdensome news that we tend to take too seriously. *Too* is the key word, for our job is to take life seriously but not too seriously. Life is a solemn matter but not a grim one.

Our days hunger to be filled with laughter and lightheartedness in order to provide perspective. We need to feel comfortable being and doing zany things, at least five minutes worth every day. I don't think most of us have to worry about exceeding the limit.

290
Shun the Deadliest of the Sins

"I matter, you matter, what goes on between us matters."
—VIRGINA SATIR

In the Middle Ages religious leaders listed seven deadly sins they considered to be the most interesting and original of human blunders. Their list holds up fairly well for us moderns: pride, covetousness, gluttony, lust, anger, envy, and sloth still remain roadblocks to spiritual growth.

Sloth is deadly because it renders us asleep, listless, and moribund. At least in the other sins we're kicking and bouncing. In slothfulness we're stuck as slow, upside down, limb-hanging, fungus-covered entities. We're mired in dejection and faintheartedness. To be slothful is to be indifferent, which, in turn, means we feel that no one, including ourselves, can make an appreciable difference on this globe.

Soren Kierkegaard, the trenchant 19th-century Danish theologian, said that "when the day of reckoning comes, there will be found a greater number under the rubric of 'the flabby' than under all the following rubrics taken together: 'thieves,' 'robbers,' and 'murderers.'" Yes, yes, and yes.

291
Bury Not Your Talents

Jesus in the "Parable of the Talent" (Matthew 25:14-30) compares the realm of heaven or the meaning of life to being given certain abilities. If we use them, we find purpose. If we abuse, misuse, or lose them, we fail to enter the realm of heaven.

We're all blessed with discrete capacities and talents. Do we show fear and hide our talents as one person does in the parable or do we exhibit faith and dare to employ them? The more we risk, the more we receive in life. There's nothing particularly complicated about that adage; nonetheless, it's ever so tantalizing to bury our beings.

We need to share our virtues and expend our talents. We are beckoned to convey rather than cloister our gifts.

292
Smiles Go and Come

"The smile that you send out returns to you."
—HINDU PROVERB

A smile requires fewer muscular movements than a scowl. A smile warms our own insides while igniting happiness in others. Of course, we're talking about real smiles, not fake ones. The same holds for gestures of genuine kindness such as embraces. When we hug another person in fondness and appreciation, we not only transmit joy, we also bring some home to ourselves. Giver and receiver are equally hallowed in the process. A yell begets a yell. One smile is likely to spawn another. That's the way optimal human communication works.

293
Soft Overcomes Hard

"Nothing in the world
is as soft and yielding as water.
Yet for dissolving the hard and inflexible,
nothing can surpass it.

The soft overcomes the hard;
the gentle overcomes the rigid.
Everyone knows this is true,
but few can put it into practice."
—ADAPTED FROM *TAO TE CHING*

The Zen master Dogen back in 1227, returning to Japan after spending many years in China with great Zen masters, was asked what he had learned in all this time away from home. And he said: "Softness of heart, softness of heart."

Our spines need to be straight as a rail, our bellies firm not flabby, our minds clear-cut and resolute, but our hearts are summoned to be gracious and sympathetic, gentle and soft without being sappy.

A sound meditation mantra and way of moving in the world is called *DROPS*: "Don't resist or push; soften!"

294
Everyone Harbors Secret Sorrows

"Believe me, we all have our secret sorrows, which the world knows not,
and oftentimes we consider people cold when they are only sad."
—HENRY WADSWORTH LONGFELLOW

We carry in our bosoms singular, piercing hurts, even unmention-
able ones. They may rarely, if ever, see the light of day, yet remain
real. We also harbor unspeakable joys: experiences too marvelous
to convey. But it's the inexpressible sorrows that seem most poignant. Our stolid exteriors sometimes camouflage our wounded
interiors.

Blessedly, we accept one another more readily when we acknowledge our own secret sorrows, even muster the nerve to share
them. True empathy is born, notes Susan Kidd, "when your tears
run down my face too."

295
Handle Traditions Carefully

"Life is no brief candle to me. It is a sort of splendid torch
which I am permitted to hold for the moment, and
I want to make it burn as brightly as possible
before handing it on to future generations."
—GEORGE BERNARD SHAW

Few things continue intact or undamaged forever. I heard of the
little girl who said to her dad one day, "Did you once tell me that

the blue vase in the front room had been handed down from one generation of your family to another?" Her father replied, "Yes, dear, why do you ask?" The girl answered, "Because, Daddy, I'm very sorry, but this generation has just dropped it."

Tradition means that something treasured has been placed in my hands, and I, in turn, am urged to pass it on carefully. Of course, once someone has gifted me with a tradition, I have the right and responsibility to handle it in my own style. I can let it be or modify it. Then, when passing it on, I must be willing to stand back and permit others to do with it as they choose.

How I receive, handle, and pass on the traditions of my life has tremendous influence on the tomorrows of my descendants. Actually, you and I possess the power to humanize or dehumanize futures. There was a recent cartoon that shows a mother and son on a ledge overlooking a nuclear waste dump. The mother with her hand on her young boy's shoulder says, "Someday, son, this will all be yours. And your son's. And your son's son's…"

296
Speak Up or Shut Up

"The greatest sin against communication is to speak when you're not moved and to fail to speak when you are."
—SCOTT PECK

On countless occasions, we blabber, out of nervousness, void of speech-ripe words, merely running on loose emotion. Conversely, times exist when we withdraw and shut up, when the floor is ours and wisdom withers inside our souls. Both behaviors block useful communication.

Albert Einstein was asked to speak at a large gathering in Washington, DC, yet he turned them down saying: "I don't have anything to say at this point. When I have found something to say that needs to be said, I will call you." Can you imagine what a better world we'd enjoy if those who have nothing to say kept quiet and those whose words we need to hear had the courage to utter them?

297
Fulfill Your Promises

"The power of a promise is the power to stick with what we are stuck with."
—STANLEY HAUERWAS

Of course, there are rare times to sever our promises, but even our broken promises might eventually be restored or renegotiated. In any case, one of life's chief lessons is to take our vows seriously at home and work, play or service.

Fragments of the vows my wife and I took 39 years ago still echo in my mind: "I promise not to surprise you except with bursts of joy. I promise to share hurts gently and refuse to match negatives. I promise to stay at our table through thick and thin. I promise to try to heal and restore our promises when they are broken."

Stand Up and Be Counted

"The hottest places in Hell are reserved for those, who, in a period of moral crisis, maintain their neutrality."
—DANTE

Times exist when we must abstain from involvement in the cause of prudence. However, in the midst of a moral crisis, when our voice is needed, we're required to stand up, speak our truths, and enact our values. When the well-being of our home or community hovers in the balance, remaining neutral is flat-out irresponsible.

When the Soviet autocrat Krushchev delivered his famous condemnation of the Stalin era, someone in the congressional hall is reported to have said, "But where were you, Comrade Krushchev, when all these innocent people were being slaughtered?"

Krushchev stopped in his tracks, looked around the entire gathering, and blurted out, "Will the person who said that please stand up?" Tension filled the Hall, but no one dared to rise.

Then Krushchev gathered himself and said, "Well, comrade, you have your answer now, whoever you are. I was in exactly in the same position then as you are now."

Our encounters aren't likely to be as momentous as this, but daily we confront opportunities to stand up and be counted for what is just or beautiful, to risk what Gloria Steinem calls "outrageous acts and daily rebellions."

299
Be As a Tree...Walking

"I see people as trees, walking..."
—MARK 8:24

Let's briefly scrutinize the various elements of the tree—trunk, bark, roots, branches, and leaves—and their relevance to the human journey.

The trunk represents the core of our being, the inner self, the soul. All that transpires in our lives must be processed through the trunk. The bark of the tree is our living, finite body. Feed your trunk with nutrients; care for your body with utmost attention.

A tree without roots (historical continuity) topples easily. Our human rootage needs to be broad and deep, receiving sustenance from various sources. The branches of our beings reach out to shelter and house various fellow creatures. They reach upward as well in gratitude and yearning.

The leaves, the flowers, the fruit—or the lack thereof—bespeak the seasonal rhythms of our voyage. There are winters and springs, summers and falls of the soul. We blossom. We are lush. We drop leaves. We are barren. When leafing occurs we celebrate our renewability. We are trees...walking.

300
Become a Star-thrower

While living in a seaside town called Costabel, the brilliant naturalist Loren Eiseley would spend the early morning hours walking the beach. He found townspeople combing the sand for starfish that had washed ashore during the night, killing them for commercial purposes.

One morning Eiseley discovered a solitary figure on the beach. This person, too, was gathering starfish, but each time he found one alive, he would pick it up and throw it as far as he could out beyond the breaking surf, back to the nurturing ocean from whence it came. She embarked on this mission of mercy every morning seven days a week, no matter the weather. Eiseley called this woman "the star-thrower."

We too are sent on missions of mercy to reach down and save, not crush, the weak…to affirm life no matter how small and seemingly inconsequential its form.

301
We Pine for Indisputable Statistics

"To the baseball-bitten, the box score is not only informative, pictorial and gossipy; it is lovely in aesthetic structure."
—ROGER ANGELL

Amid the weightiness of my vocation, I've found it imperative to enjoy the lighter, insignificant touches afforded by athletics, although as one of my sports comrades notes, "Tennis isn't a matter or life or death; it's more important than that!" For some, it's the comic strips, crossword puzzles, or computer games; for me it's baseball box scores.

In my daily universe laden with ethical enigmas and theological quandaries, it's nice to know, in one quick glance, whether my home team won or lost and how each of my favorite players did. In ministry, it's scarcely apparent who's winning or losing.

I yearn for pieces of predictability now and again, the precision of a box score, indisputable stats.

302
"I-Will" Is More Important than "I-Q"

"Upon graduation I found that there was a world that was crying, not for people who had a great deal of knowledge and wisdom, not for people who knew answers, but for people who were willing to struggle."
—ANDREW YOUNG

Andrew Young, civil rights leader, international and national statesperson, as well as trained minister, said something terribly important in this passage from his commencement charge to graduates at my alma mater Swarthmore College. In truth, we shouldn't have to wait until graduation to hear and heed this message.

As my friend says, "I-Will" is more important than "I.Q." Our society hungers for people who have learned to reason through problems and wrestle with the intractable moral issues of our epoch—who struggle to excel, struggle to love and be loved, and struggle to create enduring justice and reconciliation.

303
Keep a Sting in Your Life?

Henrik Ibsen, the Danish playwright, kept a scorpion by his desk to keep a sting to his words. I'm not the tiniest bit interested in keeping a scorpion, tarantula, or baby alligator by my bedside. They might do more than bring a sting to my words! I do, however, appreciate the sentiment.

Whatever it might take to deliver both punch and bite to our writings and tasks, we need to harbor nearby. In all likelihood, the prod will be different for each of us. We need a sting in our lives, because it's tempting to slip and slide through our days. It's tantalizing to say sweet and innocuous things, when the situation calls for a stinging reminder.

304
Grow Tired of Giving In

According to the old saying, "some people are born to greatness, and some have greatness thrust upon them." Well, greatness was certainly thrust upon Rosa Parks, though this modest seamstress found herself equal to the challenge. Known as the "mother of the Civil Rights movement," Parks almost single-handedly energized a revolution that would eventually secure equal treatment under the law for all black Americans.

From a modern perspective, Parks' actions on December 1, 1955 hardly seem extraordinary; after a long day's work Rosa baldly refused to budge from her seat in order to accommodate a white passenger on a city bus. At the time, her defiant gesture actually broke a law, one of many bits of Jim Crow legislation that caused African-Americans to suffer outrageous indignities in a racist society.

However, Parks was consumed not by the prospect of making history but rather by the tedium of survival in Jim Crow South. The dreariness had become unbearable, and Rosa Parks acted to change it. Back then, she was an outlaw. Today she's a hero. "People always said that I refused to give up my seat because I was tired, but that wasn't true. I wasn't so tired physically, because I wasn't old. I was 42. No, the only tired I was, was tired of giving in."

Every generation needs such resisters as Rosa Parks—those who are tired of being tired.

305
Refuse to Be Stingy

"When you cease to make a contribution, you begin to die."
—ELEANOR ROOSEVELT

The story is told of a queen who invited her subjects to a banquet. She told each to bring a flask of wine and informed them that the wine would be poured into a large vat. Each person mused: "What will my small flask of wine mean? I will bring instead a flask of water, and no one will know the difference."

You and I weasel out of contributing our true gifts. We bring water instead of the requested wine. We downplay our talents when the event beckons us to reveal them.

We succumb to stinginess. For life's celebration to overflow with sufficient meaning and nourishment, every one of us is charged to deliver our fair share of the load, from start to finish.

306

"Let's Start a First Stone Club..."

"Let's start a First Stone Club:
all members will receive a stone
and then see how long they can hold onto them."
—ROBERT FUNK

Funk is a biblical scholar who is referencing the stoning of the woman caught in adultery in the Christian scriptures. Indeed, as Jesus urges, let anyone who is without sin go ahead and toss the first rock at this woman. Let's broaden this admonition: in any difficult situation or overt clash, only those who are untainted are permitted to throw rocks at anyone.

A basic life-truth obtains: none of us is unblemished or clean; so our moral duty is to drop any and all rocks to the turf. Then, there exist a couple of creative alternatives: either have fun just kicking the stones around on the ground; or make up a game wherein you toss rocks toward a goal, like horseshoes; or, finally, go home and put your stones in a big pot and proceed to make some version of "stone soup" for your family and neighbors.

307

Compromise Up!

There was a young teacher who appeared for his first job interview in a rustic mountain village. Members of the school board quizzed him thoroughly on the acceptability of his views for teaching their youngsters. At last one elder asked, "We hear a lot of talk about the world being round, while others reckon that it appears to be flat. How do you feel about this?" The young man, quite anxious for employment, replied, "Well, I can teach it either way!"

This is a blatant example of weaseling. However, there are times to be a straddler recognizing the benefits of both sides of the fence. Additionally, the capacity to teach some subject matter either way—the art of creative straddling—can make us more accepting and flexible individuals. We will likely master the negatives in our own position as well as the pluses in the options we turn down.

There are compromises that forfeit our integrity, yet others may be prudent, since as leaders we need to reach different audiences at distinct times. This is what Eleanor Roosevelt called "compromising up!" Perhaps she was referring to retaining your authenticity while being pliable and yielding.

Yet when we straddle a fence, it's bound sometimes to cause discomfort to our own body and soul. So we need to be careful.

308
Sail the Straits

Scylla was a rock on the Italian coast personified by the ancients as a female monster; Charybdis referred to a maelstrom off the Sicilian coast. The sailor's job was to navigate a course between the smooth, sheer rock of Scylla and the eddying whirlpool of Charybdis, a perilous strait where the sea forever spouted and roared and furious waves were mounting up, seeming to touch the very sky. Unquestionably this marks a dangerous passage and frightful ordeal.

Yet that's precisely the nature of our human assignment: to steer routes safely between the equally awesome, inviting yet treacherous obstacles of Scylla, the rock (absolutism or rigidity) and Charybdis, the whirlpool (relativism or mushiness).

There's no real way to dodge or duck such straits, so buckle up and stay the course.

309
"Loving Leaves Stretch Marks."
—Marge Piercy

This collection of notes, quotes, and anecdotes is geared to stretch your soul. The reader is forewarned that the lessons contained herein are for thirsty, curious, and daring folks. This book will hopefully stretch your being out of its comfort zone.

Every morning I engage in a Nepalese body prayer introduced to me by ministerial sister Orlanda Brugnola. My homespun version of this ancient ritual unveils the day, keeping me on soulful track. This prayer aspires to stretch every limb of the Self. I invite you to make your own amendments to my routine, for surely that's the way of ripened spiritual practice.

Upon rising from bed, I plant my feet firmly on the floor, usually following a jaunt to the bathroom. After finding my body's center of gravity, I slightly bend my knees and cup my hands in a receptive mode, right above the navel. I affirm my core with words such as: "I am a child of the universe. I belong here. It's good for me to be alive."

Then I lift my hands, barely touching, fully stretched to the sky in a prayerful gesture, and I continue speaking out loud: "I thank You God for most this amazing day" (E. E. Cummings), or similar words of bone-deep gratitude.

When my arms reach their apex, I open wide my hands and shape them into a chalice to welcome all the manifold gifts, both challenges and comforts, to be delivered on this unrepeatable day. My words pour forth: "Into my hands are received today's delights and difficulties, sorrows and joys." Then slowly, in circling fashion, I draw my extended hands back to the beginning position, while assertively uttering: "I promise to spread these blessings to every living entity that I greet this precious day."

I repeat this ritual, perhaps three or four times, to stretch my being in ample measure. After performing this body-and-soul exercise, the day consistently tastes better.

Life's goal is stretching upward to the sky and downward to the soil; stretching in remembrance, stretching around in wakefulness, stretching toward mysterious tomorrows. Stretching, stretching, then stretching some more.

310
Strip Your Vines

"I must strip my vines of all useless foliage and concentrate on what is truth, justice, and charity."
—POPE JOHN XXIII

Simplicity does not mean naïveté or simplemindedness but *sine plexus* ("without fold"). As we age, it's a necessary spiritual discipline to shed and shred, to say goodbye, once and for all, to stuff, lost dreams, and impossible bonds—whatever it is that complicates and confounds your daily life. Let it go and let it be, so that you can move on in as simple and unfolded a fashion as possible.

That's not too much to ask of each of us, is it, to strip our vines of useless foliage?

311

You Have Ten Minutes to Live

*"Let us not look back in anger, nor forward in fear,
but around in awareness."*
—JAMES THURBER

Unquestionably, the key to a healthy and mature existence is to be as fully engrossed in every present moment as possible or, as our book title suggests, to wake up. And such deep wakefulness is relevant whether or not we have years, weeks, or moments remaining on earth.

So I ask: if you were allotted but ten minutes in which to live, how would you likely spend them?

As I reflect upon this question right now, here's my response. I would share three minutes with loved ones, one meditating upon some thought from religious literature, one minute singing, one minute weeping, another minute belly-laughing, two in quiet confession and supplication, and my remaining moments in trying to heal a hitherto frozen or fractured situation.

How about you?

312

Stay Cohesive, Hold Fast, Be Sticky and Stubborn

*"Let me tell you the secret that has led me to my goal.
My strength lies solely in my tenacity."*
—LOUIS PASTEUR

Perhaps life's secret lies not solely, but primarily, in doggedness. We can't ignore the importance of good luck and grace in attaining our objectives. Nonetheless, tenacity lies at the heart of the matter. As they say, when the going gets tough, the tough get going. To be tenacious literally means to stay cohesive, to hold fast, and to be sticky and stubborn. All the weighty endeavors of existence—partnership, parenting, vocation, and citizenship—entail tons of tenacity.

One winter when we lived in the Midwest, a neighbor was cleaning out his walk of snow when two youngsters came by, armed with large shovels. "Would you like your pavement shoveled, sir?" one of them asked. The neighbor explained that he had already made a pretty good start. "Well," said the other bold youngster, "we get most of our jobs from people who are half-way through."

313
"This Is it!"

"Nothing happens next, this is it!"
—ZEN SAYING

Zen Buddhism is the consummate religion for charging us to focus on what lies right in front of us rather than getting waylaid by nostalgia or whimsy. What is, is…so make the most of what life presents you in each unrepeatable moment. Jewish culture is framed by "L'Chaim," the recognizable call to toast life. But remember "L'Chaim" doesn't mean toasting to a good or happy life, but instead toasting to the totality of life. "L'Chaim" pays homage to the whole schmear, not merely the appealing parts.

Or back to another Zen nugget: "On bad days I'm okay. On good days I'm okay. This is called equanimity."

314

Endure Occasional Thrashings

"Nothing is as healthy as a thrashing at the proper time,
and from very few won games have I learned as much
as I have from most of my defeats."
—JOSE CAPABLANCA

Capablanca wasn't merely a good loser who never tasted the fruits of victory. Nearly a half-century ago, he was the greatest chess player in the world. So when this accomplished winner speaks of loss, one listens.

One summer past, I received various thrashings, so to speak, in different areas of my life: a rejection notice concerning a professional project, a shoulder injury that resisted healing, and a batch of unexpected tennis losses.

Not always but sometimes our lives are toughened, even boosted, because of such thrashings.

315

Express Thyself in Myriad Ways

"If I could tell you in words what I meant,
I wouldn't have needed to dance it."
—ISADORA DUNCAN

Backstage, dancer Isadora Duncan was once asked what she was trying to convey by a dance she had just performed. Her reply furnishes our lesson for today. Occasionally, we're unable to express our feelings or convictions in words. For adequate expression we need to use another mode. It's important to vary the ways in which we share our interiors: dance, pictures, touch, and more.

My parents used to remind me that as a young child I was exceptionally quiet. Up to four or so years of age I seldom spoke. Maybe I had nothing important to say. Maybe I was afraid. Maybe I just couldn't muster the words to convey my inner realm. Anyway, when I began to speak, I took off, and I've been fairly comfortable with words ever since.

Words possess the power to heal and hurt; they can bring earthlings closer together or drive us further apart. As meaning-making animals, we seek words that make us smile, open stuck doors, and allay our nagging anxieties. Perhaps a word here or a word there will do just that. But remember that something isn't accomplished simply because we resolved or even "said something."

But words aren't our sole mode of communication. There are oodles of nonverbal forms as well. I exhort you to be exceedingly inventive and versatile, exploring myriad ways of sharing your heart and body and mind.

316
When Necessary, Cling to the Wreckage

"When you're in a spot of trouble, if you swim or you try to strike out for the shore, you invariably drown. As I can't swim, I cling to the wreckage and they send a helicopter out for me. That's my tip, if you ever find yourself in trouble, cling to the wreckage!"
—JOHN MORTIMER

The title of Mortimer's autobiographical ruminations is an apt metaphor for life. Whenever we're in the throes of a catastrophe—be it accidental or self-imposed, emotional or relational—we can do one of several things to escape.

- We can try to swim to a shore that lies miles beyond our reach.
- We can wait for a ship, an unlikely prospect.
- We can cling to whatever wreckage floats in the vicinity. Then, if we're fortunate, a helicopter may spot us.

317
Become an Accompanist

There are countless soloists on the scene, even brilliant ones, but rare indeed are skillful accompanists who know their critical role rests in being background support. In jazz, musicians harmonize and help the given soloists play better; they call it *comping*.

Our world hankers for those who know how to comp, companion, complement, or accompany others. It requires an unusual knack. Accompanists tend to be unflappable.

Enumerate the ways in which you are currently accompanying other folks on life's treadmill. Then pay homage to those who "comp" you as well.

318
Accept Deferred Gratification

"I believe that a sign of maturity is accepting deferred gratification."
—PEGGY CAHN

A woman was complaining to her tailor about the delay in making a new suit. "Six weeks," she protested. "Why, the world was created in six days." "I know," countered the tailor, "and just look at it!"

Most would contend that the universe took not days but eons to emerge. Additionally, the majority of tailors work more rapidly than this fellow, but the point holds. We're accustomed to quick results. We can't stand still for six minutes, let alone six days or six weeks. Everything has to happen right here, right now. We're a culture enslaved to instant gratification.

Let's hear it for jobs well done and relationships well seasoned!

319
Be Aware of the Toilet Assumption

"I call it the Toilet Assumption—namely, the notion that unwanted matter and unwanted difficulties will disappear if they are removed from our field of vision."
—PHILIP SLATER

We are prone to decrease the visibility of social, ethical, and emotional problems. Out of sight and out of mind is our bedrock attitude. We mosey through life employing "The Toilet Assumption." Yet there remain in our past things that haunt us and hurt others until we squarely face them. There are also unpleasant tasks in our current days, which, if ignored or flushed, will cause widespread grief.

Spend moments today recalling some of those events, things, people, challenges, and unfinished issues that, while out of sight, should not be out of mind. Then be willing to invite one at a time, back into your consciousness, for an honest and healing dress down.

There Are Tokens More Precious than Gold

The particulars are private, but suffice it to say that we went with one of our family members to her recent AA meeting. She now wants her recovery struggle to go public in order to minimize secrets and to strengthen her resolve.

A few stats: she is 48 and has been in and out of recovery for the past 25 years. She has now been clean and sober two years; her birthday of choice occurs every December 16th. As she said at the meeting, "I have earned a seat in this room; I plan to keep returning to occupy this seat; but," turning to the two of us, "Mom and Dad, there are no guarantees." Clearly, our beloved daughter dwells in a state of realistic hopefulness, and so do we.

You know the Alcoholics Anonymous philosophy, "one day at a time." Well, one woman got her 24-hour-token that morning, whereas others procured tokens of 10, 20 years, and more. Drenched in tears of pride and hopefulness, I went to the clerk of the meeting and asked if I could have a 24-hour-token to stick in my wallet, as a memento of my abiding daily support for this young woman, our own daughter, and for the natural, inevitable struggles incurred as well during my own daily voyage.

She went to the back room and produced a beautiful bronze token with the words inscribed: "To thine own self be true," "Unity, Service and Recovery, 24 hours," and on the other side was emblazoned the foundational prayer of all prayers, Reinhold Niehbuhr's "Serenity Prayer":

> *God grant me serenity to accept the things I cannot change, courage to change the things I can, and wisdom to know the difference.*

I now rub that token every day as a reminder of life's fragility and our universal human connectedness. It has become more than a token; it's a touchstone for embodying all the love we humans can muster, across the miles, and spanning all the days of our journeys.

321
Be Willing to Go Two Miles

"…and if anyone forces you to go one mile, go with that person two miles."
—MATTHEW 5:41

When I was a partner in establishing a center for the homeless, there were several hard-won lessons gleaned from that frustrating yet foundational experience. Blessedly, the Center still serves the last, the least, and the lost among us in Uptown San Diego some 28 years later. Here are some of my learnings:

- We are prone, all of us who have our own home, to over-talk and under-act with regard to assisting "street people." We've got a long, long way to go to "tangibilitate" authentic and sustained outreach.

- Whatever we do to serve the homeless may seem paltry and insignificant, but it's still critical to do it. Small deeds mount up and contribute toward the formation of a culture of compassion.

- Street people were, are, and ever shall remain full-fledged human beings. They are the children of God. They are the sons and daughters of our very own humanity. They are *we* crying out to ourselves.

- The first mile Jesus is talking about entails direct service or philanthropy. Whenever appropriate, we are called—make that charged—to address the emergency needs of a fellow pilgrim.

- The second mile is pursuing not merely palliative but preventive measures. The second mile delves behind the cry for food and shelter and lifts up a person also starved for affection and meaning. The second mile includes situational counseling, information and referral, employment assistance, client support, long-range education, and legislative advocacy.

The bottom line: you and I are challenged to walk both the first and second miles with our sisters and brothers.

322
Behold an Empty Tomb!

When I was an associate campus minister at Beloit College in Wisconsin, almost 50 years ago, we did something unusual one Easter morn. When people arrived at the Dwight Chapin Memorial Chapel for the Easter worship service, they were shocked to find that the doors were locked. They couldn't get in. Amazement soon turned to dismay, and, after awhile, a bothered and bewildered crowd gathered outside the chapel, and starting chanting loudly: "Let us in, let us in, let us in!" After all, it was Easter morn, wasn't it? It was the time to enter the chapel and to celebrate the resurrection in all of its glory!

After about 20 minutes, the worshippers' frustrations turned to upset and rage. In the nick of time, our chaplain's crew, who had orchestrated the whole scenario, burst out of the chapel, yelling: "Hey, the tomb is empty, the tomb is empty. Jesus is gone. The spirit of love is on the loose, hope has stolen away, and joy is resurrected. Friends, the tomb couldn't finally contain love, hope, and joy. They're gone and circulating here, there, everywhere in the midst of our human existence! The tomb is empty!"

And then our college band paraded out of the President's house from across the street playing the popular Beatles song of the era: "Have you heard the word is love, so fine, sunshine, have you heard the word is love…?" And the streets of this serene, Midwestern campus soon were teeming with dance and song and hallelujahs, for love was truly on the loose, joy was triumphant, hope had burst free, and the tomb was utterly empty!

There are numerous ways of bursting through enclosed tombs. Sometimes a child is born, and that does it. I remember when the very day after Carolyn's beloved grandmother died another great-grandchild was born into the clan. Sometimes a seed is sown, and it ripens and grows. Sometimes a worthy cause, earlier pronounced dead, revives in another form. A heart breaks, then miraculously it comes back to life.

Yes, our human tombs are emptied in various and sundry ways.

323
Touching Can Heal

"Our pores are places for messages of love, and physical contact is very important. Four hugs a day are necessary for survival, eight for maintenance, and twelve for growth."
—VIRGINIA SATIR

The 1970s were caricatured as the decade of immediate, often bogus, intimacy. A handshake, certainly on the West Coast, wasn't enough; only a barrage of almost indiscriminate hugs would suffice. Conversely, we opened up more as a culture to the healthiness and healing available in plain old touch. We now acknowledge that our skin hungers are real, shared by all warm-blooded animals, and this universal need persists until death. As the Northern Cheyenne Indians put it: "The only way that we can overcome our loneliness is through touching."

A member of the larger San Diego community spoke to our congregation years back, relating his remarkable odyssey as a recovering (not *recovered*) schizophrenic. His main point was the cruciality of human touch: holding and being held.

As a child, you see, Joseph suffered neglect. He was ignored emotionally and physically, shuttled back and forth between his parents, lovingly caressed by neither. One cold Midwestern night there was a fierce thunderstorm, with lightning and severe wind. You know what it's like, if you've ever lived there.

Joseph was but 5 years old and terrified by the storm. He screamed out to his mom to come to his bedroom. Joseph was shaking and scared, but his mother, not wanting to be inconvenienced, hastily brushed aside his fear, with these words: "Joseph dear, hold on, don't worry; God will take care of you."

Frightened little Joseph wasn't satisfied and cried back: "But, Mom, I want, I want somebody with skin on 'em!"

324
Yeses Cost

"Being able to say 'Yes' means a willingness to pay a price."
—CAESAR CHAVEZ

No can get us off the hook, while *Maybe* places us squarely on the fence. *Yes* costs time, energy, imagination, and resources. An existence void of a Yes or a commitment will prove safe and secure but meaningless. As they say: "A ship is safe in a harbor, but that isn't what a ship is for." Without risking Yes, we humans experience modest joy or sorrow. We waddle about in the land of blah. Unfortunately, contemporary society is surfeited with yes-butters and no-wayers.

I invite us to say a bold Yes to that which matters and muster a clear-cut Yes to the persons who are precious to us. It's positively worth the price!

325
Trifles Often Aren't Trifles

"A word, a look, an accent, may affect the destiny not only of individuals but of nations. They are bold who call anything a trifle."
—ANDREW CARNEGIE

Bold isn't the word I would use here. Arrogant or foolish seems more to the point. Expansive lives are usually lived by those who treat the trifles as decisive. They dignify the details. They play inconsequential parts with enthusiasm, what Emerson called "leaping lightning." They treat every word, look, and accent with utter respect. They know that any given moment may turn lives around, and they want to be present when transformation occurs.

326
"I Recovered My Tenderness by Long Looking."
—THEODORE ROETHKE

We appear fatigued, jaded, and brittle. Where is the tenderness in our souls?

We often bring it back by an active gaze and a level glance at the whole of reality.

We look long at the beauty of a foreign mountain or a familiar face. We look long at our choices and our discards. We look long at our daily menu. We look long at our roots and our wings. We look long at our own trials and tribulations as well as those of our neighbors. We look long at what previously caught only a passing gander.

"Long looking" means calming down and taking our spiritual pulse.

327
"Trouble Keeps Coming."

"I am not at ease, nor am I quiet, nor am I at rest,
for trouble keeps coming."
—JOB 3:26

Clearly, there's trouble to avoid, but there's also trouble to instigate, like fighting for justice or restoring a fractured bond or saving a wounded animal. This sort of trial or turmoil is what one activist calls "necessary" trouble. How one handles or creates such trouble is a prime indicator of the size of our humanity. For as Rita Mae Brown put it: "People are like teabags—you never know how strong they'll be until they're in hot water."

Albert Camus in his novel *The Fall* writes about the dungeon cell in the Middle Ages called the "little ease which was not high enough to stand up in nor yet wide enough to lie down in. One had to take on an awkward manner and live on the diagonal. Sleep was a collapse and walking a squatting." Well, that's pretty much how life seems sometimes, doesn't it?

There is dis-ease, un-ease, and little-ease in being human. Trouble, of every sort, is integral to being alive, so we need to grow accustomed to it, skirting the wrong kind while fostering the right kind.

328
Admit You May Be Wrong

"My friends, by the bowels of Christ I beseech you, bethink you that you may be mistaken."
—OLIVER CROMWELL

To admit "I may be wrong here" or "I was mistaken in what I just did" are therapeutic admissions that spring us beyond haughtiness. Are you and I strong enough to admit how mistaken we are sometimes? Here are but three examples:

- Charles Lindbergh was not the first person to fly nonstop across the Atlantic. He was the 92nd, although he was the first to do it alone.
- And did you know that a "red flag to a bull" doesn't mean a thing, since bulls are color-blind?
- And one more. The Emperor Nero didn't fiddle while Rome burned, since fiddles hadn't been invented, plus he was 35 miles away at the time of the fire.

In Zen, there is one thing you must possess above all else, if you are a seeker after Truth. "I know, I know what it is," exclaimed the disciple to the Master. "An overwhelming passion for the truth!" "No," the master replied, "a readiness to admit that you may be wrong!"

H. L. Mencken, a polemical genius, whose hate mail has probably never been equaled for vituperative juices, used to answer all letters, however malicious, with a postcard on which was printed:

Dear Sir or Madam:

You may be right.

Yours, H. L. Mencken

At other times, we need to realize that a lengthy retort would be wasted. All we can do is offer a Menckenian note: "You may be right." This keeps us genial and our respondents puzzled.

329

We Are Unfinished Animals

"Here's a test to find whether or not your mission on earth is finished: if you're alive, it isn't!"
—Richard Bach

The most significant thing you can say about human beings is that we're incomplete and unfinished. We remain unspecialized, ever learning what is necessary to survive and adapt under varying conditions.

Our jobs are unfinished too, as reminded by the Talmud: "Do not be daunted by the world's griefs: love mercy and walk humbly. You are not obligated to complete the work but neither are you free to abandon it!"

Thomas Merton closes his autobiography with the words: "*Sit finis libri, non finis quaerendi*" or "Let this be the end of the book, not of the searching." Yes, indeed, our quest continues; the road leads onward. So, I reckon the key to a fulfilling, not a finished, life is to keep on approximating our ends, keep on inching ever closer toward the justice, the beauty, and the love for which we eternally ache.

330

"Vengeance Isn't the Point; Change Is."
—BARBARA DEMMING

This is sobering counsel for a society that features getting ahead, getting back, and getting even. In partnerships we frequently seem set on vengeance rather than change. We want to be "right" rather than "happy," let alone "healthy." We seek to score points rather than make the game more humane. The same pattern obtains in the business world and in political organizations. And surely religious and international communities aren't exempt from the disease of retaliation.

For our relationships to heal and our jobs to develop, nothing less than change is required. And change, the real article, demands intentional alertness and effort. Easy is not another name for constructive, thoughtful change. Conversely, vengeance may appear to be a tempting response but surely one where both sides lose.

331

Produce a Little Cadenza

Clarinetist Artie Shaw, popular in the Big Band days, in reflecting on his life as a musician said: "Maybe twice in my life I reached what I wanted to. At the end of 'These Foolish Things' the band stops, and I play a little cadenza. That cadenza, no one can do it better. Let's say, it's five bars. That's a very good thing to have done in a lifetime. Artists should be judged by their best, just as athletes are. Pick out my one or two best things and say, 'That's what he did: all the rest was rehearsal.'"

It's refreshing to know that the best in their chosen fields know that they rarely reach their summit. The most productive artists all experience pedestrian performances.

Yet each of us also can produce, once in awhile, a cadenza that showcases the pinnacle of our gift.

332
Be a Gatekeeper

A colleague reminds us that Yin His was the keeper of the gate in the Great Wall of China and refused to let Lao Tse pass until this sage had written down his wisdom. The result: the classic *Tao Te Ching*! This encounter, said Peter Scott, marked one of the important points in human history.

It takes courage to be a designated gatekeeper who dares to challenge, perhaps even rebuff, folks at key junctures in their journeys. Every community needs its necessary contingent of police officers geared to protect and serve the citizenry. Such agents of "surveillance" are essential to the well-being of society. We could also use more self-appointed gatekeepers who intuitively yet bravely know when to pressure fellow beings into birthing the best of what dwells inside their minds and spirits.

Three cheers for Yin His and his ilk.

333
We Seem to Be Verbs

"I live on Earth at present, and I don't know what I am.
I know that I am not a category. I am not a noun.
I seem to be verb, an evolutionary process, an
integral function of the universe."
—R. BUCKMINSTER FULLER

Along with Fuller, I envision us to be verbs, creatures of verve and vibrancy, action and assertiveness, growing. Yet, too often we aren't verbs at all, but nouns, static substances, or adjectives, always modifying but seldom moving ahead under our own steam. Then again, some of us are conjunctions or prepositions, providing valuable links between entities.

You can't have a sentence without verb. Life pales without them too.

334
We Are Only Visitors

An Hasidic tale relates a tourist from the United States visiting the famous Polish rabbi Hafez Hayyim. He was astonished to see that the rabbi's home was but a meager room filled with books. The only furniture was a table and a bench. "Rabbi, where is your furniture?" asked the visitor. "Well, where is yours?" replied Hafez. "Mine? But I'm only a visitor here." "So am I," replied the rabbi.

You and I are but earthly visitors, for spells of different lengths, so it would be prudent to make ourselves at home, wherever we've currently landed, being surrounded only by resources that we need, and always remembering that we're merely passing through.

335

Ditch Cynicism

You know about the cynic who declares: "Blessed are they who believe in nothing for they shall not be disappointed." Or the cynic is one "who looks both ways before crossing a one-way street." Or "give an inch, and they'll measure it." And the epitaph upon the tomb of the cynic reads: "I expected this and here I am."

Contrast the cynic's negative demeanor with Robert Louis Stevenson's sense of determined hopefulness: "I believe in the ultimate decency of things. Aye, and if I woke in hell, I'd still believe in it!"

It's not a question of who's right or wrong, the hopeful person or the cynic. It's a matter of which manner of living maximizes joy and meaning for you and your fellow travelers. Go ahead, make your daily pick!

336

Listen to the Voice Within

"The more faithfully we listen to
the voice within us, the better we will hear what
is sounding outside."
—Dag Hammarskjold

Our lives are polluted by an incessant stream of noise. We are inundated by a cacophony of sounds. We need to return to what the Hebrew scriptures call the "still small voice" or "a sound of a gentle stillness." The writer of Kings is referring to an eerie stillness that can be heard. We could all benefit from more such moments of exquisite quiet. Then we will be better equipped to entertain the sounds of our external world, selecting those relevant to our well-being and screening out the ambient clatter and clamor.

337
Exude Radiance

St. Thomas Aquinas spoke of beautiful things as having radiance. What an exquisite word. "Radiance" refers to experiences of splendor and objects that radiate brightness. Radiant people exude love and confidence; they shine, and we bask in their light. Artists like Renoir who painted a sun-bathed vision of human life shed a luster of vision on canvas that delivered sparks of joy to the viewers as well. Cartoonists such as Walt Disney lubricated our oft-dreary lives with magical mice, flying elephants, Snow White and Happy, Grumpy, Sneezy, and Dopey—fantasy characters of an imagination that left us glowing for the visit.

All sorts of phenomena can manifest radiance. When we are moved by a smile or a piece of music, by a spoken word or a magnificent deed, we're basking in radiance.

Religion, if I'm not mistaken, consists in locating radiance, spreading radiance, simply being radiant.

338

Dare to See and Be Seen

My friend, Joe, always delivers a special retort upon being greeted. I start with "Hey, Joe, it's sure good to see you!" And he replies: "Tom, it's good to be seen, very good indeed!"

Such constitutes the essential and necessary exchange among both individuals and institutions, make that countries as well. Our job is not only to truly see folks–eyeball-to-eyeball–when we engage them, but also to allow ourselves to be seen in return, and then to acknowledge the fact that we've been truly seen.

Once we see and are seen, then an authentic bond can be forged. Indeed, once we stay in practice, we're far less likely to leave any child behind, leave any youth unseen, and leave any adult unheard.

339

"Practice the Scales of Rejoicing."

Bach reported his music training as the effort to "practice the scales of rejoicing." Whether you play an instrument or hammer a nail or kick a soccer ball, every activity available to humans requires, for its fulfillment, that we practice the scales of rejoicing.

It's told that the Swiss psychologist Carl Jung suffered from a mid-life identity crisis. He recovered his sense of direction by constructing something out of stone with his own hands, because as a child he had been happiest on the timeless afternoons he spent building sand castles.

The way out of depression is often to press outward or to produce something. It's early, but our 10-year-old grandson, Owen, is as he puts it, "addicted" to *legos*. Whenever Owen squirms at wit's end, he builds, sometimes for hours, with his *legos*, amusing both his hands and his imagination.

Have you discovered your own version of building sand castles or legos? How are you practicing the scales of rejoicing?

340
"God Worketh Hitherto, and I Work."
—JOHN 5:17

Conventional theology has emphasized human sinfulness and divine perfection. In short, we pump up God's image while degrading our own. God is venerable while we are villainous. Humans botch things up, but the Infinite Spirit somehow sticks around to pick up the pieces.

Many of us are uncomfortable with this simplistic assessment, because we believe humans to be necessary partners with God in celebrating and sustaining the created order. Our human labor is neither insignificant nor unessential. It's integral to a holy partnership.

On the one hand, God banks on our becoming responsible stewards of the universe, and, on the other hand, we have faith that God will be able to carry its/her/his fair share of the freight.

That reminds me of the story of Ethan Allen, the American patriot, who, after the capture of Ticonderoga, hurried home to his family in Vermont, and, while there, attended a Thanksgiving service. Town history has it that during the long prayer in which the Rev. Dewey was giving all the credit for the victory to the Lord," Allen interrupted: "Parson Dewey, Parson Dewey!" At the third call, the minister paused and opened his eyes. "Please," said Allen, "mention to the Lord about MY being there!"

Heaven and earth, divine and human—both powers and presences are required.

341
"The Gods Frustrate Us in Two Ways..."

*"The gods frustrate us in two ways: by giving us what
we desire and by not giving us what we desire."*
—George Bernard Shaw

Sometimes we reach our goals yet remain unhappy. Usually this occurs because we celebrate madly, our egos inflate, then, unless our ambition stays vital, we vegetate. Once we feel we've "arrived" in anything, we're likely to grow moribund. The flipside is that the gods also frustrate us by keeping us from our goals. So if our desires aren't met, then we're prone to moil around in resentments or self-pity. Either way, we're aggravated.

So I suggest two things: (1) accept that frustrations are built into human existence; (2) face head-on every persistent frustration, get over or through it, and move on. Like Moses we will never reach our Promised Land. The best we can do, and it will prove sufficient, is pass the torch on to Joshua who will visit and dwell in the land of our sought-after hopes and dreams.

But don't be surprised if Joshua will be periodically frustrated there as well.

Be Wary of Near-Enemies

"In Buddhism near-enemies describe traits and efforts that look like earnest steps toward right being and action, but they are actually counterfeit enticements, which, in the end, only derail and deflate us."
—MARK NEPO

This is a concept that draws subtle yet crucial distinctions for our days and nights. Here are a few examples: pity is the near-enemy of compassion, apathy of acceptance, modesty of self-loathing, and bravery of foolhardiness.

Here's a poem I wrote in 1991, echoing the same sentiment:

Beware virtues revved a notch
Imperceptibly glide into vices
Examination slithers into over-examination
Woman's assertive edge turns acerbic
Man's newly acquired gentleness goes mushy
Children's earned independence runs amok
Country's glorious principles are compromised
Religion shrinks into pieties and decrees.

What would make your list of near-enemies?

343

Practice Benign Deviations

"My deviations are benign. I am a pacifist, a vegetarian,
a Catholic trying to be a Christian, a union member,
a bicyclist and a runner."
—COLMAN MCCARTHY

Deviating simply means diverging from the crowd, nothing more and nothing less. In other words, being your own person. In reviewing your life choices, can you discern which of your habits, even passions, might be nontoxic and which are deleterious to self or others? Our days become easier to plan when we attempt to eliminate our offensive deviations and practice the benign ones.

Plus other folks naturally benefit when we negotiate this critical distinction.

344

Note Your Omissions

Rabbinical wisdom says: "We will have to give account on the judgment day of every good thing which we might have enjoyed and did not." Unfortunately, morality is often seen merely as a code of prohibitions, which, if rigorously obeyed, will guarantee entrance into heaven. The truth is larger than that. The ethical life is more problematic.

One can eschew negative behaviors and fall far short of a good, let alone, abundant life. We must be as concerned with our omissions as our commissions.

Be vigilant today: there are some important, even breathtaking, things awaiting you. They have your name on them, waiting for you to celebrate them. Don't ignore or shun them.

345
We Are Sometimes Loved Despite the Evidence

"We should all have one person who knows
how to bless us despite the evidence."
—PHYLLIS THEROUX

We need a friend, partner, parent, or counselor to whom we can go and unabashedly say: "Here I am, blemishes, holes, and all—I need you to accept me as I am!" That's the essence of the Prodigal Son story.

The younger son squanders his inheritance, ashamedly returns, and "while he is yet at a distance," physically afar and psychologically marred, the son is accepted by his father. He is embraced, contrary to any earnings, despite any evidence. The prodigal son is blessed and made worthy by the love of the father.

In truth, the father turns prodigal too, that is, lavish and overflowing in love.

346
Bring a Dream to Fruition

One of Bach's pupils once asked him: "Papa, how do you ever think of so many tunes?" to which Bach replied, "My dear one, my great-

---

est difficulty is to avoid stepping on them, when I get up in the morning!"

Naturally, few of us are blessed with the prodigious talent of Bach. For some, it's tough merely to dredge up a couple of melodies per week. Nonetheless, every one of us, in some fashion, is a creative visionary. Probably our greatest difficulty isn't a surplus of great notions but adequate discipline to realize a few.

If every week, we could envision, corral, then bring to fruition one dream, we would be creators par excellence.

347
A Long Journey Begins with a Step...

Fifty years ago, on October 1, 1962, James H. Meredith, previously barred from entering the University of Mississippi because he was black, enrolled at the university as the town of Oxford became embroiled in violent riots. Meredith displayed courage. He challenged prejudice. He took the craggy yet pivotal first step towards justice. Growth for his race, for all Americans, occurred because of James Meredith's noteworthy act of moral bravery. A long journey begins with a step. Sometimes a courageous step.

Certain aboriginal peoples engage in a beautiful practice by speaking the same first phrase to all newborns: "We love you and support you on the journey." At their memorial the deceased hear the very same words: "We love you and support you on the journey."

Such life-affirming words need to be spoken and heard not only at the start and end of our earthly stints; they would prove invaluable all along the pathway.

348

"See Everything, Overlook a Great Deal, and Correct a Little."
—POPE JOHN XXIII

Life invites us to juggle three acts.

- We need to "see everything": be alert and accessible to the whole of life's flow. In other words, wake up, have all your antennae up and working.
- We need to "overlook a great deal": be magnanimous, ever-forgiving. Instead of being quick to judge, we would do well to practice patience and forbearance in all our relationships and vocations.
- Finally, we need to "correct a little": offer advice only when called for and counsel that will improve the conditions of all concerned, not merely assuage our own anxiety.

349

Spend Time Shaping Your Middle

"Millions who long for immortality often don't know what to do with themselves on a rainy Sunday afternoon."
—SUSAN ERTZ

As the saying goes: destiny may shape our ends, but we alone must shape our middles. This little mantra exudes multiple meanings, including sensitive weight-watching, but the main insight is piercingly clear.

How and when we come into the world was not our choice

to make. How we close out our existence is usually beyond our control too. And what we'll actually do during eternity remains an unknown. Therefore, the key is what we accomplish between the parentheses of birth and death, during the interval of our given earthly life.

Do we mindlessly fritter away the middle moments or do we intentionally mold them with our own hearts, hands, and heads? Let us be brave enough to handle what truly lies within our grasp on both sunny and rainy afternoons.

350
Waiting Counts As Real Time

December especially harkens a month of fundamental impatience, a season of racing and dashing rather than pausing and pondering. To be sure, we're not constitutionally unable to wait, at any age. We're able to inch up to the holidays: count days, keep secrets, slow down, and soak in sounds and songs.

There's evidence that we can wait: aren't some of our earliest and fondest memories those of waiting: waiting for one of our parents to come home from work on Friday afternoons, knowing we might be going out as a family; or waiting with other kids in line for a Saturday matinee movie; or waiting around on the sandlot for our after school game to start; or all costumed and just waiting to go trick-or-treating in the dark on Halloween? Yes, we all have a history of productive and enjoyable waiting.

Waiting isn't provisional time; it's valuable per se. Waiting gives us a chance to brood creatively. We wait so that our souls can catch up with our bodies, so that the rhythm can take shape before we start to dance.

We wait during December so that inner events can unfold in

the midst of all the outer hoopla. For the true gifts of the holidays, of life itself, aren't external but internal, if we but wait patiently and allow them to be born.

351
"Walk Beside Me and Just Be My Friend."

"Don't walk in front of me; I may not follow.
Don't walk behind me; I may not lead.
Walk beside me and just be my friend."
—ALBERT CAMUS

There are moments to lead and times to follow. Nevertheless, real friendship finds folks most frequently sharing steps and stories alongside one another. As the legend goes, we were born not from either the foot or the head of Adam but rather from the rib. Why? So that woman and man would not be over or under one another but remain willing and able to walk side-by-side.

That truth also holds for woman and woman, man and man, as well as adult and child. And let's expand the wisdom to include work associates, races, orientations, and nations. The mantra "walk beside me" obtains for all earthly creatures.

352
"Be Candid Beautifully."

"Speak tenderly to Jerusalem."
—ISAIAH 40:2

Soft-spoken and mild-mannered, the American bishop Joseph Bernardin had a knack for achieving goals without causing undue rancor. A top Catholic cleric said in admiration: "When Bernardin makes waves, they're always smooth." A teacher of mine in seminary said that there would be times in ministry when you must share painful, abrasive truths. Do so in a soothing fashion, he urged. I have never forgotten that advice, whether sitting across from a parishioner, my wife, a community activist, an opponent, or our neighborhood children.

It is wise to speak softly when saying something harsh. As Kahlil Gibran phrased it: "If you must be candid, be candid beautifully."

353
Describe the Contents of Your Wallet

When I've sought to get to know young teenagers better, deepening our mutual bonds, I've called us together after a meal and songs. While sitting on the floor, I've invited every one, as we so choose, to empty the contents of our respective wallets or purses. I call it "wallet theology," because what resides in your wallet tells the world a whole lot about what you hold dear.

In my wallet are photos of loved ones, cash with which to make "smart choices," and odds and ends that are dear to Carolyn and me, such as a scrap off a napkin from one of our early dates. There are also cards that denote membership in clubs ranging from the Memorial Society to my local magic ring. There is much more as well.

What do you keep in your wallet? And do the children and youth who pervade your life actually know what you cherish?

354

"Weep and Begin Again."

"Perhaps if I had a coat of arms, this would be my motto:
weep and begin again. "
—Mary C. Richards

We all want to begin over, but we tend to bypass an essential prior step. We need to say "goodbye" before saying "hello." We must purify our systems as much as possible before launching something fresh. Weeping, literally and figuratively, is perhaps our optimal cleansing agent. It always furnishes a "watershed" moment. As the Desert Tradition invited: "Look, weep, and live!" You can't argue with tears; they always matter, emanating from a deep place. As my friend Doug von Koss invites: "Don't wipe off your tears; let them tumble to the ground and grow something!"

I find weeping everyday to be a spiritual practice of great import. When I weep through the smaller, relatively easier transitions and losses, it prepares and keeps me in sound shape for more complex and agonizing passages.

In the Jewish heritage, tear cups are placed on your living room mantel. When you return from daily labors, you proceed straightway to the mantel, take off your glasses and deposit your accumulated tears into the respective cups of sadness, joy, and confusion as well as any other cups of your personal choosing.

The amount of water you release into the diverse cups is the measure of your day's humanity.

355
Speak Your Life Out Loud

"Everything becomes a little different as soon as it is spoken out loud."
—HERMAN HESSE

Things happen to our thoughts as they emerge from the safety of the mind's cavity. First, it seldom comes out like we think it will. Public expression takes on a life of its own. Out loud we can ramble, sputter, or sometimes sound funny. Second, when spoken, our feelings have a chance of being misunderstood or mangled. Third, once our words are uttered, they can not be retrieved.

Speaking can prove to be a gutsy, even heroic, act; for it involves risking losses as well as reaping dividends.

356
Watch Out for Whatlessness

Theologian James Luther Adams tells a story about the Harvard geologist Nathaniel Shaler. To the great annoyance of numerous colleagues on the faculty, Shaler persisted in objecting to the award of a top scholarship to a certain student. Repeatedly Shaler was reminded that this student possessed an all-A record.

Finally, another professor put the question squarely to Shaler: "Why are you set against this person who has such a superb record?" In reply, the tall, red-bearded Scotsman arose and said: "I am voting against this student because of her cantankerous *whatlessness!*"

Shaler was protesting against the emptiness of so much learning. Some students, as they say, drink at the fountain of wisdom while others just gargle, no matter how sterling their grades might be. Being brilliant means nothing unless one's intelligence is utilized in the service of the larger truths of beauty and love, joy and justice.

Some scholars, in all fields, suffer from "whatlessness"—a lack of depth and dedication, then pass that disease on to their students.

357

"Comfort the Afflicted and Afflict the Comfortable."

*"It is the duty of the press to comfort the afflicted
and to afflict the comfortable."*
—H. L. MENCKEN

It is not only the duty of the press to do the aforementioned duties but also the mission of families and government to heed Mencken's advice. Our highest yoked tasks are essentially to support one another in sorrow and to goad one another in complacency. Furthermore, both jobs need to be accomplished on a routine basis, sometimes with the same person during the same day.

The art consists in knowing when to do which with whom, since the needs vary in our lives. In others words, become an ambidextrous person.

358
Make the Necessary Alterations

"We must alter our lives in order to alter our hearts; for it is
impossible to live one way and pray another."
—WILLIAM LAW

Whether counseling people or dealing with my own blocks and
burdens, I admit to being an unrepentant behaviorist. I pay close
attention to feelings and attitudes, but ultimately lives are changed
through actions. If we're afraid of something, emoting and reflecting are beneficial, but real transformation occurs when we confront our fears. Action is the best antidepressant. All else misses the
mark or falls short.

Today, I invite you to make some alterations, however modest,
with your clothes, pathways, dreams, and relationships.

359
May Beauty Crowd You

"Beauty crowds me till I die, beauty mercy have on me
but if I expire today, let it be in sight of thee."
—EMILY DICKINSON

Beauty not only surrounds or crowds us, it sometimes actually enters us. Beauty pushes and tugs away at our very eyes and innards.
Our prime job is to turn around and meet beauty, salute it, and
then join forces with it.

Emily Dickinson increasingly withdrew from the world to become a full-fledged recluse. Nonetheless, this superlative poet, all dressed in white garb, would lower baskets of treats, tied with a rope, from her second-floor balcony straightway into the eager arms of children waiting in the street below. And, of course, hundreds of Dickinson poems were found later in her dresser drawers, which would bestow bountiful beauty upon us all.

Beholding or creating beauty lights our inner fire. It sets our souls ablaze. Beauty can even nourish the capacity to become bolder, better selves. Artistic pleasure doesn't necessarily produce a more responsible citizen, but the potential remains present. Our mission is to embody Plotinus' sage phrase: "Those who behold beauty become themselves beautiful."

And when our day runs its natural course, may it conclude in the sight of beauty.

360
Just Keep Breathing

A woman celebrating her 100th birthday was interviewed on television. The anchorperson asked, "To what do you owe your longevity?" "Nothing to it," the woman replied. "Anybody can do it. I just keep on breathing."

Breathing is the bridge from body to mind. It builds up the lungs, strengthens the blood, and revitalizes every organ in the body. Eastern religious philosopher Alan Watts used to say that the curious thing about breathing is that it can be evaluated both as a voluntary and involuntary action. I am doing it, yet it is happening to me.

The key to a fruitful, fulfilled existence is this: make breathing your best buddy. Breathe and let breathe!

361
Choose Your Place of Burial

There's a sad, rather grotesque, fact about the legendary Lebanese poet, Kahlil Gibran, who was buried in a setting similar to that of a second-rate saint. Romantics, like myself, loathe this story, but we've got to face the multifaceted truths about our heroes and heroines.

Gibran is buried in a gift shop. He lies in state, the coffin covered with plastic flowers, counters on either side hawking souvenirs, in an old monastery at Bsherri in the highlands of Lebanon. Gibran abhorred the cheap and the superficial, the ugly and the fake, so it's ironic that such was his fate. Only intellectual snobs would gloat, saying that a sentimental, popular poet deserves a grave in a souvenir shop.

I personally find Gibran's poetry and prose on death, partnership, and children profound not shallow. They have always furnished foundational readings for my selected rites of passage as a professional.

In planning your own last rites, where would you choose to be buried?

362
Refrain from Zapping One Another

"Ouch, no zaps; when upset, say ouch.
Zaps are denunciations."
—SHARON WELCH

In short, whenever you feel hurt, vent an "ouch," yelp a bit, then retire awhile, readying yourself, when appropriate, to deal with the person who delivered the blow. The problem with zaps is that you're trying to retaliate or wound someone. You are turning the other into an opponent. Zaps can convert a solvable scrap into an extended battle, where there are no winners, only losers.

We could do worse than follow the counsel of Jesus in Matthew (summing up the 613 laws of Leviticus) when he encourages us to "reprove our neighbor"—that is, correct one another with kindly and gentle intent.

In sum, whenever you're irked or hurt, I implore you to have direct dialogue. An honest ouch–plus a hearty conversation–seem about the right combination.

363
Wag Your Tails!

A charming story describes how the Christian scriptures were translated from English into the Inuit (Eskimo) language. Problems arose for the translators when they encountered certain words in English for which there were no corresponding terms in the Inuit language. For example, there's a passage that tells that the disciples are filled with joy upon meeting Jesus. But since there is no word for "joy" in the Inuit language, the translator had to find another way to express the meaning of the passage.

In their research, they discovered that one of the most joyful times for an Inuit family is when the sled dogs are fed in the evening. The dogs come barking and yelping, bounding about and wagging their tails energetically. The children squeal with delight, and the neighbors join the frivolity as well.

Consequently, the translators used that particular event to help convey the meaning of the aforementioned biblical text. As a result, when the passage was translated back into English, it read: "When the disciples saw Jesus, they wagged their tails!"

There we have it. Our earthly assignment is to bark and yelp wildly, gamboling and wagging our tails as furiously as possible, so that our joy might prove contagious, and all creatures of the universe might clap their hands, sing and dance, joining in life's perpetual celebration.

364

"May Life Wonder Me!"

"I did not ask for success; I asked for wonder and you gave it to me."
—ABRAHAM HESCHEL

The "you" here could be a friend, God, or any living creature. I take it to refer to Life writ large. If success were all I acquired during my days, then existence would be wearisome. My failures and losses, while painful, are seldom ruinous. I've needed them, most of the time. How about you and yours? Whereas success isn't an imperative, wonder is. My life would be downright impoverished if void of a rousing sense of awe.

There is a story told of geography students having toured the earth by book, who were asked at semester's end to list what each considered the Seven Wonders of the World. Though there was some disagreement, the following garnered the most votes: Egypt's Great Pyramid, the Taj Mahal, the Grand Canyon, the Panama Canal, the Empire State Building, St. Peter's Basilica, and the Great Wall of China.

While tallying the votes the teacher noted that one student, a shy girl, had not turned in her paper. "Did you have trouble?"

the teacher inquired. "A little," the child replied, "I couldn't quite make up my mind, because there were so many."

"Well, tell us what you have, and maybe we can help," the teacher suggested. The bashful girl rose to her feet and began, "I think the Seven Wonders of the World are to *touch* and to *taste*, to *see* and to *hear*..." she hesitated, "and then to *run* and to *laugh* and to *love!*"

May our souls never harden to the marvelous, the magical, and the miraculous. Or, as the Pennsylvania Dutch say: "May life wonder me!"

365
Have It to the Full

"I came that they might have life and have it to the full."
—JOHN 10:10

Having life per se isn't sufficient. The challenge is to "have it to the full." Flourishing, magnificent, resourceful existence is what our living is summoned to be. When we have abundant life, right here and now, our journey exudes joy and spreads justice. This biblical admonition exhorts us to get pleasure from a zesty time on earth!

Literally, zest constitutes the thin outer skin of an orange or lemon that can be used as flavoring in whatever we eat. It also translates as an enjoyably exciting quality or piquancy of life. It reminds us to relish life and conduct it with mucho gusto.

Delineate ways in which you lead a full and zesty existence with your mind, your body, your heart, and your spirit.

366
Punctuate Your Life with an Amen!

I grew up thinking that the term Amen meant "so be it," as if we were merely adding an exclamation point to what had just been spoken or sung in community. I have since learned that Amen correctly translates "so *might* it be." Amen refers not to an actuality so much as to a hope.

Therefore, when I voice an "Amen" in private or public, I am, in effect, pledging to do everything possible to help my sentiments reach fruition. Amen isn't another sweet, superfluous four-letter word thrown in for magical measure. Amen is a promise to translate our yeses into deeds that might heal and empower the cosmos.

Amen.

Afterword

After compiling my lessons, I happened upon this most beautiful and apt Kabir poem. You may also discover that once you dwell in a spiritually attuned and awakened state, all sorts of inspirational nuggets seem to capture your attention. They may not literally say "Wake Up," but they will call out to you personally, having a wake up effect.

Wake up epiphanies and experiences will seek you out. And they will find you. May it be so.

My inside, listen to me, the greatest spirit,
    the Teacher, is near,
    wake up, wake up!

    Run to the teacher's feet—
    who is standing close to your head right now.

    You have slept for millions and millions of years.
    Why not wake up this morning?
    —Kabir

Kabir, the son of an Indian Moslem weaver, lived in Benares during the 15th century. His spiritual growth was deeply influenced by Sufi poets and Hindu Vedic teachings.

Index

About Tom Owen-Towle

The Rev. Dr. Tom Owen-Towle has been a parish minister since 1967 and is the author of two dozen books on personal relationships and spiritual growth. Tom and his life-partner, the Rev. Dr. Carolyn Sheets Owen-Towle, are the active parents of four children and seven grandchildren. Tom is a guitarist, parlor magician, tennis player, and currently sings with seniors, mentors children and youth, and volunteers with San Diego's homeless. Owen-Towle is a national leader who continues to conduct workshops and retreats on the core themes of his books.

You can contact Tom at:
3303 Second Avenue
San Diego, CA 92103
www.tomo-t.com

Aperion Books

Book Publishing for the Digital Age

Aperion Books is dedicated to producing high quality publications that help people facilitate positive change in their lives. We specialize in publishing titles on spirituality, wellness, and personal growth.

Our unique Collaborative Publishing Program is specifically designed to help writers and authors expand their personal and professional horizons through creatively designed books that are distributed to national wholesalers and leading retailers.

CPSIA information can be obtained at www.ICGtesting.com
Printed in the USA
BVOW031337050213

312450BV00002B/253/P